A Thousand MILES —TO— FREEDOM

A WORLD WAR II ESCAPE MEMOIR

MARTIN KARI

Copyright © 2025 Martin Kari.

All rights reserved. No part of this book may be reproduced, stored, or transmitted by any means—whether auditory, graphic, mechanical, or electronic—without written permission of both publisher and author, except in the case of brief excerpts used in critical articles and reviews. Unauthorized reproduction of any part of this work is illegal and is punishable by law.

ISBN: 978-1-63950-380-3 (sc)
ISBN: 978-1-63950-381-0 (hc)
ISBN: 978-1-63950-382-7 (e)

Because of the dynamic nature of the Internet, any web addresses or links contained in this book may have changed since publication and may no longer be valid. The views expressed in this work are solely those of the author and do not necessarily reflect the views of the publisher, and the publisher hereby disclaims any responsibility for them.

Writers Apex

Gateway Towards Success

8063 MADISON AVE #1252
Indianapolis, IN 46227
+13176596889
www.writersapex.com

A SIGNPOST

The hell is empty, the devils are amongst us.
—Shakespeare

History teaches us that it teaches us nothing.
—Voltaire

Humans made me to like animals.
—Schopenhauer

Nobody is guilty of what lies in the past, but remains responsible that it won't happen again.
—concentration camp survivor

CONTENTS

Dedication vii
Chapter 1   Start of War Imprisonment 1
Chapter 2   First Transport Collection Point 3
Chapter 3   Change into Railway Wagons 5
Chapter 4   Russian Border 9
Chapter 5   Railway Journey into the Unknown 11
Chapter 6   End Station in Siberia 15
Chapter 7   Task - Coal Delivery from Underground 19
Chapter 8   A Day in the Concentration 24
Chapter 9   Winter & Christmas 27
Chapter 10 Braking Away from the Straitjacket 29
Chapter 11 Escape Steps 34
Chapter 12 Paysans Stick Together 40
Chapter 13 Finding the Railway Line Again 53
Chapter 14 How to Get on the Train 58
Chapter 15 Necessity of a Disruption 61
Chapter 16 Back into the Train 68
Chapter 17 A New Disruption 73
Chapter 18 First Encounter with a Town 78
Chapter 19 Regular Departure with the Train 88
Chapter 20 Saratov - Belgorod by Train 91

Chapter 21	Belgorod, a New City Encounter	95
Chapter 22	First Border Crossing into Ukraine	100
Chapter 23	First Encounter with Home Country	104
Chapter 24	Border Crossing Moldavia - Romania	111
Chapter 25	Arrival in Kleinschelken	117
Chapter 26	Way Separation Doesn't Stop	123
Chapter 27	Regain Kleinschelken	125
Chapter 28	Busteni, A New Way	128
Chapter 29	Notifications from the West	132
Chapter 30	South Africa	136
Chapter 31	Brazil	138
Chapter 32	Europe & Transylvania	139
Chapter 33	Kleinschelken Again	142
Chapter 34	"Escape" from Kleinschelken	146
Chapter 35	Jurisdiction in Romania	149
Chapter 36	The Further Way	151

DEDICATION

For Arja,

My compass through every storm, My constant light in the darkest nights, and the quiet strength behind every word I write.

When this story was only a flicker of memory, you believed in it — and in me — with unwavering faith. You carried its weight when I could not, and you reminded me that even the coldest landscapes can hold warmth when love is near.

Your patience gave this book its breath; your kindness gave it its heart.

Through every late hour, every doubt, and every silence, you reminded me that stories of endurance are not only written about the past — they are lived, every day, by those who love without limits.

This book is for you, and because of you.

With all my love,

Martin

START OF WAR IMPRISONMENT

When the rooster crowed early in the morning on the dung hill, the weather was a mixed bag for a change on that day. However, on the twenty-second of June in 1941, the cock remained silent and here is why.

After a promising spring time, summer had moved into Transylvania (Siebenbürgen) with its balmy, longer days. Although bad news about the war from the neighbor's radio continued, Michael, the winegrower , would go on foot to his small field, which he could still call his own at the time, at sunrise every day. To get there, he had to cross the road and the deeply washed out riverbed of Kockel.

A quick look at his wife, Sara, reassured him that he could briefly look after his business. An unease already overcame him when he arrived at his small field because his wife was expecting their second child.

When Michael decided to return home, he encountered an unusual military patrol only a short distance from his home. A handful of men dressed in uniforms not known in Romania . They didn't even speak the Romanian language but were sounding like Russians. Michael was ordered to take the hoe off his shoulder and lay it on to the side of the road. All this was enforced by the command, "Put both your hands up, and don't move."

It was difficult for the winegrower not to understand the command, *ochotska*, which means, "follow us". The gun pointed towards Michael only reinforced such a command. Even the plea, "I can't leave my wife alone. She is expecting our second child" couldn't change the mind of the soldiers.

FIRST TRANSPORT COLLECTION POINT

Michael encountered other neighbors cramped together like a cattle herd in front of the local Kleinschelken church fortress.

There were no words; only silence reigned. A military truck never seen before in this small village picked up those frightened villagers. No questions were asked. One thing became obviously apparent: No small children were among this crowd. Instead, villagers from Kleinschelken of a mixed group showed up without belongings, just wearing the clothes they were dressed on.

The presence of the arms silenced the villagers. A frightened woman held her daughter close to her arms. That didn't prevent a soldier from snatching the daughter and loading her on to the truck. The mother begged with tears in her eyes, "Please don't harm her. When you have a family of your own, even you wouldn't like to see a young person's life destroyed."

What happened afterwards remained anybody's guess. Meanwhile, the peasant Michael was given no time to recognize known faces. Women remained hidden, covering their beautiful hair as much as possible to look more like men. In such a situation, women were especially endangered.

The number of villagers didn't seem to be large, which helped to load them quicker on to the military truck with or without assistance.

The big wheels of the truck gave its passengers the shivers, as the stony road with its holes allowed it. This crowd found itself along the truck's interior on the opposite wooden benches. There were also armed military personnel on board, who nobody knew or recognized. It was impossible to think that under these conditions, somebody could even have the slightest thought of escaping from the truck if they valued their life.

Where everything was heading from then on, remained to be seen, but the daily hours didn't wait for that. More and more people met in military trucks from close by to farther away on such a path of uncertainty.

How could this have happened? Another war again! The Second World War caused these events, and Romania had to deliver its "contribution" with the prisoners of war. Who was next in line? Transylvania, of course!

The German forces couldn't be helpful at that time. Russia enforced its military might. The transport out of Kleinschelken arrived at the district capital, Mediasch, before dusk.

The peasant Michael was already preoccupied with how to get out of this hellhole.

He was fully aware that an escape could cost him his life. The duty officers had their guns ready to shoot. Michael didn't want to abandon his plan to escape. His thoughts went in one direction: Only time will tell. He was certain that the price of this undertaking will not be cheap.

CHANGE INTO RAILWAY WAGONS

They arrived at the railway station of Mediasch. Carriages were waiting in a row on the railway sidelines. A two-wing sliding door could be seen in the middle of each carriage where a door led to both sides. A small platform connected each carriage.

Trucks, with their human load, stopped on the side of each sliding door, where spaces were available. Michael, the peasant from Kleinschelken, didn't show signs that there was any problem at home, where his wife was in need of help.

How could such an uncertainty be beneficial for anybody? *What have I done to face this situation? God help me please !* Michael implored silently. Given the situation he was in, Michael felt like he was on destiny's swing, where the life goes forwards and backwards, often even up and down.

Michael was holding his breath as best as he could, neither happiness nor hope could be seen in his face. Even if he had known what was going on at home, he could have done nothing. Is this how fate can sometimes catch up with us, even for a short time without any hope?

Michael, the Kleinschelken peasant's second son was born on the same day without his knowledge. His wife, Sara, suffered the worst possible fate—death—as proper care was not available on that day when Russia invaded Transylvania.

How this newborn second son, Martin, could continue his life still remains an unsolved mystery.

As a matter of fact, Mediasch, the district capital, became a starting point for both the father and the son. Transport train carriages took care of the father, Michael; whereas the son, Martin, is said to have found temporary accommodation at the local orphanage.

Back to Michael in Mediasch where the crowd of locals were kept behind one another so that each could pass one at a time in front of a table next to the carriage. In this process, only a few locals were selected to assist as long as they followed the demands of these occupying forces, naturally, without a gun.

On lists of paper appeared the details of these locals who were now the prisoners of war. The next move was that these new prisoners of war were guided, one at the time, to a sliding door of the carriage. It was up to each prisoner how to climb through the open sliding door onto the timber floor. Problems following these instructions were handled in a strict and short manner. Nobody was left behind.

The advanced hours of the day reminded everyone to hurry up the process so that the train could still start its journey before dusk. The weather of this summer day, at least, supported this move. More support of any kind stayed hidden. Finally, from somewhere, a steam engine turned up, ready to pull this "freight" away. Where was it going? None of the train prisoners had any idea, probably not even the officers on duty. What became evident was that the armed foreign soldiers had taken the position on the protected small platforms between the carriages but not before the sliding doors of all carriages were closed and securely locked.

Ochotska now became the mission's name, which the train passengers could not have the slightest idea yet. Regardless of that, the train departed, leaving Mediasch behind to bid farewell to the sunset and the surrounding high, sharp, pointy Carpathian Mountains.

What was before the bumpy road for the trucks now became the regular interval of the railway line from one rail to the next one, similar to, "Ho, ho, rider, when falling he cries, falling into a hole, eating him the crows." Nobody was in such a mood! With the diminishing daylight, the prison carriages lost their light coming through small windows at the platform ends, giving more time to think about something.

Could it have been possible that everybody had one and the same thought? Nobody was ready to follow it. To highlight such a situation became an important task, to put into words what kind of feelings prisoners of war and their relatives and friends left at home could express. It is a noble task for an author to serve the truth.

Most of all, there was uncertainty on board the train carriages. Questions about eating, sleeping, or visiting a toilet was, on the train, no issue. What were the answers to these?

For the time being, the carriage wheels rolled without interruption throughout the whole night. As long as the military control on the train was convinced that everything was in order, everything remained quiet.

There was plenty of time for the prisoners to think, either voluntarily or mandatory. Michael joined the others in total silence. Despite the fact that even under the poor light that entered the carriage, he knew most of the people around him.

Before the complete darkness took hold, the soldiers in charge on the little platform between the carriages had put up a lantern on the ceiling, from where a tiny light entered the carriages.

What can I possibly do when my hands have been tied together? I can't do nothing else than open my "box of memories," Michael thought. *If this isn't not enough, God help me, I beg Him for that.*

Nobody had any idea what time it was. In such a moment, the time remained at home. A shimmer of daylight penetrating the carriages was all that allowed a guess of the time. Many hours must have passed since the train once stopped from the start of that journey.

Where are they now? That thought crossed the minds of the approximately twenty-five passengers. Only much later, their exact number became obvious to these trapped prisoners of war.

RUSSIAN BORDER

From outside, voices from an exchange of words penetrated into the carriages, not only Romanian words were spoken but also strange ones. Based on their accent, they must have been Russian words. To surmise from this, the train must have arrived at the Russian border. This gave the first indication to the passengers where this journey was heading.

Meanwhile, hunger and thirst couldn't wait to announce their presence much longer. In addition, to use the toilet was only possible under the strict military control. All this was already enough to justify a stopover. The time for the stopover depended much on the military supervision.

No wonder that none of the passengers could get their most urgent needs satisfied. Tschai, a warm black tea, with a small slice of bread prepared hungry stomachs for only a foreseeable future. Somebody who could speak a little Russian received an additional slice of bread.

A continuation of this journey was certainly not forgotten. It was also made sure that all passengers were back on board. The military supervision personnel were exchanged on regular intervals. They were not considered for Siberia. The supervision ensured no complaints or any misery came to their attention. And if so, only a passenger who was near death or dared to resist was removed from the train and taken officially from the passenger list.

So far, everybody was at least spared the gun. Caution was also the mother of wisdom. How much could wisdom satisfy hungry stomachs?

Every new departure into a new day required a stocking up of the steam engine's coal and water. There was a maintenance person on hand. The wheel-connecting rods received a good lubrication. The experienced maintenance person also checked the wheel hub caps with a knock on them, making sure everything was still in place.

The daily routine covered also the necessary visits to an outside toilet in a tiny timber hut, strictly accompanied by the military personnel. Afterwards, every prisoner of war had to pass a wooden table in front of the carriages to receive what barely helped to survive for the moment. It is still a well-known fact that hungry stomachs follow better than satisfied ones.

RAILWAY JOURNEY INTO THE UNKNOWN

As this journey continued, Michael became more interested where all this might end and how long it would take before somebody would give up. Therefore, it became inevitable that one poor passenger finally had enough of this kind of suffering and expressed his anger loudly. This would not last for long because the military personnel arrived straightaway.

Who was now made the scapegoat? The prisoner of war, or the military personnel, or the organisation that used the political voice? Were circumstances or something else responsible for all this? How much did people really differ despite their different roles in daily life?

Independent consideration can only teach us that manpower corrupts characters no matter what. Material benefits and superiority also play the role here!

How much could these prisoners of war have been aware of their fate with this *Ochotska Siberia* remained to be seen. Everything didn't need to be bad even there.

The farther northbound this journey went, the longer the sun shined. At least the weather was, for the time being, kind towards the prisoners of war. The few people who met outside appeared well-minded. Mainly, uncertainty kept them away from the train.

When word about the coal came up, nobody could possibly have known that mining was waiting for the prisoners in Siberia. It was definitely not a laughing matter that the carriage right behind the steam engine was loaded with coal from prisoners of war.

Besides all this, only a quick look at a Russian map would have given a frightened impression of the distances. Short after the Romanian border, endless forests, mountain ranges, and tundra plains opened the space starting around Kyiv, Saratov, Chelyabinsk, Omsk, Novosibirsk, Tomsk until the far away small place of Tura in Siberia, which still has not ended.

According to the swing of life with its constant change in motion from forwards to backwards then ups and downs, in Russia always counted, "the Czar is far away."

Distances change still rules today Russia. One rule here was the mission transporting the prisoners. A close eye was kept officially on it, in between was free-play available, which the prisoners of war had to deal with. The time, this journey was left to coincidences. Only at its end, a more clear picture emerged of how long this journey had really taken, of course under the condition that sunrises and sunsets were counted correctly. One could again have asked here is who was here the originator? Of course, like always, somebody else here unknown!

According to the distances and the present travel conditions during the summer, this journey must have taken three to four weeks. In the middle of winter, such journeys could not take place.

How could the peasant, Michael, from Kleinschelken manage this "mission"? Time for reflections on this situation was more than enough. Now comes the question: How could this be helpful at all? Michael didn't stop, however, to forge in secret his plans to get out of this situation. Whether or not the other fellow sufferers could possibly have made their mind up in a similar way, it was kept in the dark.

Regardless of all these considerations, the train kept going northeast, through day and night, bound for Siberia .

Russia planned to bring development to Siberia considering its size, not forgetting its demanding location especially during severe winter months that reaches far into the north. To do so, prisoners of war were the ones to carry such a burden. Nobody was asked to answer who started this fight because war time ruled again. To deliver an answer had a too bitter taste for innocent bystanders like the prisoners of war. Out of all these, a depressing boredom took hold of everybody in the carriages, even the military personnel were not excluded.

In an even rhythm, the wheels responded monotonously to every rail connection with a banging sound. It was left to the passengers to get along with time. For instance, to look straight ahead for five minutes then eventually back and look to the left and right, as well upwards and downwards.

Could something like this help to prevent people on board this train to go crazy? Nobody was spared from outbursts during this journey. The longer this lasted, the more its inmates understood that with precaution, the darkness in the carriages could be overcome by communication. It could only happen slowly as the guards were listening to maintain order and discipline.

Surprisingly, out of the darkness and silence, words could help this situation. Close neighbours from home recognized it suddenly, even in such a cramped position. Don't hurry, but remain cautious became the order of the day. Only a few words already had that effect and pulled some people out of a deep low, restoring them with new hope, some power even for moments. It's also known that constant drops of water wear away even a stone, which means that what can last will succeed. Such a simple recipe assisted to overcome the lean periods for the ones who could gain strength from it. Food and help were not enough to get out of a low. Words often work wonders when they find sound ground.

Which day of a week this journey had reached became increasingly unknown. The silence in the beginning of this journey changed slowly but surely into a cautious exchange of words, sometimes also with a helping hand. All this happened during the days in semi-darkness and nights in complete darkness.

Hope resisted, however, all these challenges that also this "mission" will find an end. Small things like water to wash hands or even to dream about a shower did not exist. Practices to survive were first of all required. One of them became inevitably to tighten the belt a bit more every day, if conditions allowed it. People from the countryside had to cope with less difficulties. At the end of this "mission", these prisoners of war could count what was left from their bones and skin.

END STATION IN SIBERIA

To avoid difficulties, understanding this text could become boring like a train journey. The author gives a little more "free play" to reach a happier end. The end of this railway journey must come closer after so many difficulties. More or less, every passenger had turned clothes into rags. Hair was not exempted either. They stuck up on heads, showing in all directions. No smell was noticed anymore.

When the end station finally came, nobody wanted to remember its name. Many of these prisoners of war could get out of the carriages through the middle sliding door only with the help of the others. The distance from the timber floor of the carriage to the outside was almost a person's height, causing considerable difficulties for most of the run-down prisoners of war. But where there was help, there was also a way.

Despite a solid ground under the feet, the legs didn't want to move yet. The stops in between until the end-station differed mainly in size compared with the local towns. In a bigger railway station, the train stopped only for a short time where the security measures were more visible.

The shrinking sizes of fir trees resulted also in a smaller number of locals. The area turned increasingly wider and more open, which also indicated that Russia showed its size in less populated areas as well. In bigger places, people were more crowded there.

This end-station became a nightmare when the Russian polka music from an accordion tried to revive spirits of the prisoners of war. Nobody was in a mood to dance to the accordion's tune. These completely exhausted new arrivals were not ready for such a doubtful welcome, even when it came from local Siberians who lived more or less a solitary life.

Where to go from there? This became the closest question as soon as the railway carriages were abandoned. Meanwhile, the military personnel kept a constant close eye on the prisoners of war with a gun, who stood in a row next to a timber hut that resembled all the others around.

A few public officials in uniforms kept themselves busy listing the new arrivals. Before anything could go further, each prisoner of war received a bandage with a number on the right upper arm. In an addition, the left forearm received a blue number bandage. The hand signs to the left and right by the officials indicated neither to damage nor take away the numbers. The number was now the main identification.

A path through a gate led to timber huts, which were surrounded all the way by high solid wire mesh. Whoever needed help with walking could surprisingly count on it for the moment. The explanation for it was a simple one: Whoever was able to walk was also useful for work. This way none of the prisoners of war was left behind.

A certain number of these camp inhabitants were allocated into waiting timber huts. Men and women were separated to keep trouble out as much as possible. Camp beds on top of each other across a timber hut also offered a blanket as a place to sleep.

Ordinary timber tables with the exact required number of chairs found place where the camp beds left enough room. Last efforts helped also Michael to get into one of the barracks, which looked like a bed, that was waiting for him. Before going to bed, the number on the bed had to match the prisoner's blue number on the wrist. The question turned up: What was greater, the hunger or tiredness?

A control person in the barracks decided that hunger was greater. The prisoners of war also called barrack occupants were freely given the task to look after themselves, to pick up a steaming hot soup from the pot in the barrack kitchen nearby. A few slices of bread and plates added by the guard next to the pot.

Hunger now became overwhelming, while the strength was already dwindling. A soup ladle was not supplied; therefore, it was left to everybody to shovel soup with another empty plate into one's own plate. The steam from the soup pot followed the plate quickly enough so that the bottom of the pot showed only some pieces of food. Swimming bubbles of fat became visible on the top of the soup. Luckily, nobody was aware of this because nobody was in a hurry. Scooping soup from the fat came with the instructions: Be cautious. The soup is hot. Don't burn your mouth.

The desire to have at least something warm in the stomach left every individual to find out just how hot the soup was. However, to call this near and good enough remained a distant option.

Meanwhile, the day didn't stop to continue its path. Where the loo was located didn't require any special instructions. The smell already pointed to the direction. Therefore, it was better not to be too close to it. A water tank in its own timber building was protected from the severe winter's condition, finding also its place between the timber barracks.

Then, the first night in a prisoners' camp finally happened, away from the notorious rattling railway wheels. Light remained scarce, only with armed supervision personnel who remained hidden in designated places during the night.

Michael from Kleinschelken followed orders without opposing anything. He now had something to call a bed for himself. It was better than the hard wooden floor planks in the train carriages. Dreams during his first night were still of home with worries what was happening there.

Here, no rooster announced the early morning. In the late summer, the sun still shined daily in Siberia for many hours. Even during the night, the sun didn't disappear completely. The light then looked in a thin crescent still over the horizon.

The first visitors on arrival were inevitably the mosquitos. They ruled in Siberia in such great numbers that there was no escape, turning into one of the major challenges in a Siberian prisoners' camp. Attempts were however made to keep this plague in check. Smoke from bitumen torches wrapped carefully in hay sent smoke into the air, keeping the mosquitos partly at bay.

Siberia has, by the way, the highest temperature differences in the world during the year. In the summer, temperatures around thirty degree Celsius are very common; whereas during the winter, the temperature can drop to minus sixty degree Celsius.

Even as this vast land was and still is sparsely populated, people must know how to survive. Permafrost also calls its home here. That means the frozen ground never melts completely during the year.

Conifers, for that reason, don't grow tall here, remaining more flat near the ground. Worth to mention is also the huge amount of gas trapped near the surface. For such a reason, coal mining is performed only deep underground in shafts.

TASK - COAL DELIVERY FROM UNDERGROUND

During that time, prisoners of war were also taken to Siberia to extract coal from underground. While men performed shift work around the clock, women worked most of the time in the camp. If any strength was left with the prisoners, it became a necessary practice to work together and not against each other to gain only small advantages. In real terms, there was nothing to gain; everybody was equal even the military personnel.

In the beginning of a work shift, men from the barrack had to line up in a row outside and report to the supervisor their camp number. The same happened at the change of a work shift. A short break was then included. While one shift mined coal underground, another one loaded it with a shovel into wagons on the rail stationed underground, too.

Men had to tackle the task of the transport to the underground on their own through a downwards shaft on a simple platform hanging on ropes and rollers, an engineering work of art that nobody would have been concerned about! Women, on the other hand, would also learn how to twist sheep wool with their fingers from a wooden spindle into useful thread that could be used to knit socks, mittens, caps, jumpers, including trousers and some made these out of animal fur for a better protection against the cold. Skilled as well as less skilled hands helped each other without asking for it to bear this difficult situation better together. Pressure to compete was out because there was nobody else to compete with.

Even words found their way gradually to an exchange. Women, particularly, were endangered by abuse. As long as it didn't become obvious, everything stayed silent because there was nobody to keep record of what was happening.

After a rather short autumn season in this northern part of the world, its display of color turned out modestly because deciduous trees (trees with leaves) couldn't gain a foothold here. The long lasting cold Siberian winter waited everybody without an exemption.

Before this time, everyone was asked to prepare everything as much as possible for the winter. Coal mining was high in demand, like everything else, to deliver the much-needed warmth. Timber as well as coal must have been collected by the war prisoners with their own initiatives to keep the ovens in the barracks heated.

Once the winter has taken hold of Siberia, there was no escape from it—no car, nor train, nor aircraft at that time anyway. They all were hampered in the Siberian cold with the snow on top of it. Life was then put on hold. However, not in the war prisoners' camp. A far away forged plan dictated that prisoners of war had to be kept busy, so nobody could have any chances to step outside this order. The cold took care of it already. A demanding but not forgiving nature had limited human activities and still is doing it today.

Michael from Kleinschelken followed blindly like everybody else but still worked secretly on his escape plan. He also remained very careful when it came to a change of shift in the coal mine. Michael observed this process from a distance, who was in charge, and how it was handled. There is a reason why it is commonly said that everything needs its own time, and this was no exemption.

In the barrack, which was mainly housing people from Kleinschelken, everything remained quiet and, so far, under control. Something could be heard out of neighboring barracks every now and then. Nobody was seemingly interested to take notice of it. The main thing appeared was that calm returned. As the winter came closer and the cold increased, everybody became more occupied on how to survive this challenge.

The everyday life established itself in the camp. Michael avoided being called to the coal mine. Safety was not an issue here. It was dependent on every miner to get along for their own safety. Already at the entrance of the mineshaft, enough challenges were waiting. For instance, the ropes on the platform during their move downwards required brake action by hand so that it couldn't go down too quickly. This task was left to the prisoners of war who were on the mine duty. How they handled this "technology" was entirely left to their responsibility, so nobody else could have been held responsible for any mishaps.

Going down can happen often easier and quicker. To control this became the task as everybody was keen to get out of the mine shaft again, preferably alive.

When the platform suddenly came to a halt with a bang gave the indication how far it went down. A mine representative already waited there with instructions where to go that day in the underground labyrinth of the mining shafts.

At least one advantage showed there: The cold lost its bite underground. Half in the dark, illuminated only with protected lamps, a main shaft tunnel led to where coal was broken out of a vein.

The shaft tunnels were supported by strong wooden beams in a regular distance so that no shaft could easily collapse. These beams had to come from far away, farther south, because not even conifers could take a foothold in the Siberian permafrost area.

A bigger danger than the collapsing of a shaft were the hidden gas pockets in and around the coal veins. At least during his prison camp time, Michael did not experience any gas explosion in the mines.

Small rail lines for trolleys were also waiting underground for the miners. At the end of a shaft tunnel waited a number of trolleys to be loaded. Pickaxes were lined up on one side of the shaft tunnel and shovels on the opposite side. This all was under a strict supervision of a mine representative who carried a gun ensuring that pickaxes and shovels were only used for the mining work underground.

Once down in the mining shafts, the miners had to start without delay and break the coal first out of the vein with a pickaxe by hand. The cold was still felt down underground, but it was not cold enough for the sweat to appear on miners' bodies and faces. It could not be denied that working horses need food, and if it was out of reach, both work and worker would suffer.

As soon as a good amount coal was pickaxed out of the vein, another group of miners moved in with their shovels, uploading the coal into the waiting trolleys.

Even for technically minded people, this kind of transport system had to be an eye-opener. Naturally with time, control around the coal mining lost its efficiency as the prisoners of war miners were constantly kept busy, to the extent that no questions nor answers could get hold on either side. It looked almost impossible that somebody could even have considered to escape from such a "straight jacket". The exemption will, however, prove with a weak point in the system that it could still happen.

At least for the time being, everything went smoothly as much as the eye could see in the prisoners' camp. As soon as the piled up coal was removed, the shovel miners extended the rails closer to the coal vein. Michael was not overly keen to work hard. The work was done in a way so that the supervisors had no reason to complain.

Michael's native peasant craftiness also enabled him to watch everything closely because the more frequently something was done, the less attention it will receive. For the time being, this meant to cooperate and not to swim against the current but run with the pack.

Michael also preferred the job with the shovel, because breaking the coal out of the vein with a pickaxe was not only exhausting but also involved much black dust in the air, inevitably marking faces and hands.

The daily target of coal production with three working shifts was three complete filled up trolleys. To push the full trolleys on the rails to a collection point could only be done with the rest of a remaining strength. At their destination, other miners were busy shovelling the coal out of the trolleys into baskets mounted onto a transport band which another team was winding by hand up to the top. Another horizontal transport band also moved, by hand, the coal away from the shaft onto a considerable pile of a coal collection.

When it came to clean yourself after a day in the coal mine, each barrack held, on a table in a corner, a few bowls of water. Only in this place somebody could try to get rid of the black coal dust. One piece of soap had to help with the cleaning for a whole week. Additionally, something that was said to be used as a towel also helped the cleaning process. After much use, these towel-rags ended up on a string going across the corner to, hopefully, get dry again for another shift's use.

A DAY IN THE CONCENTRATION

A few women were appointed for the task to maintain fire in the ovens from which the curved pipes went through the ceiling into the outside. The ovens were fed with coal and branches cut to a fitting size. A pot, with only a few unrecognizable ingredients, waited on the stove to be heated and served as warm soup.

Hunger was the best cook here. Tiredness, on top of it, never failed to be a steady companion. As soon as the stomachs of shift workers were a little satisfied, the camp bed became the next choice. Only the quietness that followed allowed thoughts to develop more freely in a prisoner's head. It depended how much time the shift work left during the day. Some tried to gain, out of these moments, something what could still have made sense. For instance, the exchange of words with other sufferers worked wonders or even a long overdue cleaning helped, and last but not least, to sometimes play games with simple materials alone or in the company of others. All this was limited to gain distance from a seemingly hopeless situation. Neither drinking nor smoking was on because nothing was available. It must have been more difficult when the surrounding duty officers played openly excited music.

Michael, the peasant from Kleinschelken was thinking that this show could only add to a less reduced attention in their duties. His plan to escape from these conditions had to be very carefully and secretly prepared without risking his life. In his understanding, it was best not to talk to anybody, not even a single word.

Time didn't stop to move despite the beginning of winter and its great challenges. It didn't escape the prisoners' memory that Christmas was coming. Some of them were counting the months, weeks, and days, carefully discussing it with a few others. Winter brought with it, Christmas, a quiet time. The snow stopped with the extreme cold. The coal mining also stopped when the temperature reached negative forty degree Celsius. Everything moved slower when it was cold, even underground in the mine shaft. The supervisory staff then turned, more or less, a blind eye to what happened.

Michael became aware of this, too. As far as the attention allowed, he continued in secrecy to build on his plan to get somehow out of this. The whole camp fell into a kind of hibernation the closer Christmas time came. Even the control attention almost stopped. The wide-ranging camp fencing remained shut, only used by the shift changes of the control bodies at its openings. It also appeared obvious that nobody would leave the protection of the camp. Something unknown waited there far and wide in the white scenery of Siberia, too.

Enough efforts were already necessary to keep the situation in the prisoners' camp alive. The longer winter was around, the more the prisoners of war had to rely on their own. People suffered many hardships, especially during the winter, that nobody dared to think or act outside the commonly known limited possibilities or impossibilities. This situation helped, however, the prisoners became closer to each other from the fear of the unknown.

Basic help was the first thing everybody could still remember: how to make a bed with help, the need to get dressed up, wash oneself with the little that was available, maintain fire in the stoves within the barracks, collect timber branches and more coal in an exchange with a number of camp colleagues, maintain cleanness and order as much as possible. This was the only way a positive attitude could be upheld. At least it did appear that nobody had reached the stage of giving up hope because the commonly shared hardship kept everybody together.

Meanwhile, Christmas came closer. In the communist Soviet Union, Russian Orthodox religion was officially abolished. Despite that, to believe in something higher and better remained in people's mind, particularly throughout the vast isolated areas of Siberia. An orientation away from the "hard hands" throughout tsar-times—the incredible Stalin-rule, the successors of communism—they all have lost ground here with distance and time. Only much later in history, did Soviet Union President Gorbachev bring back religious orientation with the Orthodox Church. During World War II, religious orientation never lost ground; it remained a steady companion in the hearts of people who experienced, in these difficult times, a rejuvenation in a belief during the cold of winter. The repeated good efforts to reconcile with the bad through a strong belief.

WINTER & CHRISTMAS

Fir tree branches together with handcrafted simple candles' lights allowed the camp supervisors to turn a blind eye because they also secretly kept the Christmas tradition in their minds and hearts. Also, storytelling changed from one camp prisoner to another while they moved closer to each other around the few round tables in the spaces that were left between the camp beds. A Christmas melody on their lips for whoever could remember them.

Memories of home moved many of them to tears, a remainder of joy in the eyes.

The prison supervisor was officially prohibited by his superiors to show any compassion. A task that also held them unconsciously imprisoned. The question remained: Why were people here imprisoned? Many could have asked this question on the war prisoners' side as well as on the side of the Russian authorities. How good or bad was the world here? The answer to such question remained, voluntarily as well as unconsciously, unanswered in Siberia.

Back to reality: Around Christmas in December, the fewest daylight could be seen far in the north. Around midday, this semi-darkness was shortly interrupted by pale light streams on the horizon which continued reflecting farther on the white snow surface.

Silence reigned over the camp and work was kept on hold; protection against the severe cold became more important.

War prisoner Michael, more determined than ever, had come so far with his plan to free himself, under any circumstances, from the shackles of being a war prisoner. A move, however, that still remained highly risky. Michael made this clear to himself during the long winter months, thinking constantly about it.

10

BRAKING AWAY FROM THE STRAITJACKET

On Christmas Day, not during the coldest hours, Michael took his destiny into his own hands and escaped from the prisoners' camp in Siberia. It was the cold that kept the guards in their cabin. In memory of Christmas, vodka helped raise the atmosphere, too.

Michael used this distraction to start his escape. The fenced gate at the entrance was shut but not locked. Michael had recognized it a couple of times before, and now he had the courage to creep flat cautiously on the ground through the small gap of the gate. Michael had won over the dog in the guard's cabin with daily bread crumbs so that the dog had no reason to become alerted.

Outside the camp fence, Michael had to get away as quickly as possible through the obstacle of the deep white snow. For a short distance after the camp fence, Michael covered his foot prints with a branch that he moved across behind himself. His chances of being discovered were least likely.

At least at this moment, Michael experienced a taste of freedom. How free was he really? As quickly as possible, he had to leave the few houses next to the camp without drawing unnecessary attention. The bitter cold was already enough to keep Michael to move fast.

After a certain time, the reduced number of guards on the Christmas duty must have smelled a rat because the dog wanted to go outside without its usual warning bark. *Somebody should go and have a look at what is going on there,* came to the mind of one guard. He went out into the cold, not without his shotgun by his side and the fur hat on his head.

The dog remained inside the camp's gate and didn't indicate that something was amiss. However, the guard picked up something suspicious while he looked farther past the fencing. At the gate, still in the vicinity of the camp, the searchlight showed somebody disappearing into the darkness of the night. Without hesitating a moment, the guard pointed his gun into the direction of where Michael had started his escape. A big bang went three times into the direction of the suspected fugitive. However, the searchlight didn't reach far enough to find out whether the fugitive was hit and had stopped him from escaping further.

As soon as Michael saw the guard with the shotgun, he immediately laid flat on the ground and continued to crawl with all his strength, almost submerged in the snow. This effort and the three gunshots accompanied Michael through all his life.

Michael changed his name immediately to Igor, a more Russian sounding one. In real terms, it was only a matter of time that it was also officially recognized who was missing in the prisoners' camp. It became most pressing for Michael or Igor to gain distance from the camp. (Before his escape, the prisoner of war used the name Michael and then Igor everywhere else after the escape.) Never before nor afterwards did Michael strain his efforts to such an extent in search for freedom.

What happened from then on in the prisoners' camp became less important for Michael. He had to concentrate on everything in his power to get away from this past because he was well aware enough of what would happen if he was intercepted.

After gaining a good distance, the peasant Michael from Kleinschelken found refuge with a peasant in Siberia. Nobody saw him;

therefore, he could remain unchallenged. All the efforts in such cold were extremely demanding. Only a strong determination could handle this situation. During this first effort to escape, Michael had nothing else on his mind than to gain distance as far as possible from the camp.

The timber house of a Siberian peasant stood isolated in a vast surrounding area. Michael approached, watchful of the farm house. As he only he could have expected, a dog barked first. The dog must have realized that Michael was in a difficult situation. Soon after the dog's barking, a person came out of the house. Now the moment had arrived that Michael could convincingly show his friendly nature.

Meanwhile at the prisoners' camp, the camp's control officer convinced himself that at least one bullet from his gun had hit the escapee as nothing could be seen and everything remained silent. The thought that tomorrow will be another day for a closer inspection, crossed the control officer's mind, and it was better for him to return to the warm hut as it was right in the middle of the night and too cold to be outdoors.

The next morning, it was the rule that only one officer went outside the fence surrounding the camp. After a few steps through the deep snow, the officer convinced himself that the escapee could not have come far enough in his escape, even if a bullet had hit him or not. Alone, the cold must have slowed him down so much that he could not have gone far enough. In addition, the dog made no effort to follow a trace in the snow. What the control officer didn't know was the previous short encounters with Michael and the dog where they got to know each other better. This way the escape was a hair's breadth in front of the camp control.

In the end, the officer preferred to go straight back to the hut within the prisoners' camp as no trace of a fugitive prisoner could be found. To get rid of something in this cold could have waited for a while longer. The rule, however, dictated that a lost war prisoner was taken off the camp's list at the least. To find out the prisoner's name was left better for later on.

A peasant knew certainly best to communicate with another peasant, even when different languages made an understanding more difficult. What also helped in the absence of words was friendly expressions can work wonders with the support of gestures and sign language.

Back in the prisoners' camp, Michael used the little time available to pick up Russian words, which helped him divert attention away from the misery more commonly surrounding the other camp inmates. Now that the time arrived when all these achievements, no matter how small they might have appeared at the time, became a touchstone for Michael.

How good or bad it was that the camp location was not even marked on a map remained an open secret. Here did matter : Nothing ventured means that nothing was gained, which, however, required craftiness, power of wisdom, perseverance, and lots of luck. Michael was fully aware of this even subconsciously. The requirement was to catch up with every situation that led to the road to freedom.

Michael with luck already on his side with his first stopover at a farm house in complete darkness. No difficulties were waiting for him. No wonder who wanted in these harsh winter conditions add more problems to the already existing ones? Michael was, in any case, well advised to keep his stopover, which was still too close to the prisoners' camp, as short as possible.

Michael demonstrated his willingness to cooperate by offering a helping hand to the elderly couple in their cow shed by cleaning the corner of the two cows first with the pitch folk, followed up with a hard broom, and afterwards lay out dry fresh hay on the ground. The two cows had no objection; they happily wagged their tales. Only a few molasses came at a time into the feeding trough because it had to last throughout the whole long winter.

As a sign of recognition for a helping hand, the elderly couple shared their small warm evening meal with their "guest" at one and the same table.

This short break had to be enough for Michael as he had to gain more distance away from the prisoners' camp. The farmers must have known about the circumstances why Michael turned up in their place. Simply out of humanity, they didn't want to put more burden on him than he already had. The understanding was, therefore, equal on both sides that Michael wanted to keep going as soon as possible despite the bitter cold outside. The couple had nothing to say for their own security reasons. They were convinced that this sudden visitor must have known what he was doing.

How many of these stopover visits will Michael experience? He couldn't know in advance. One step at the time reminded Michael of it. This only will enable him to manage the huge distance homewards, which still lay in front of him. In the obscurity of the darkness, it felt much safer because hardly anybody would have tried to stop somebody in an escape during the cold Siberian winter.

ESCAPE STEPS

After one stop was achieved, stop number two would follow. Each step forward had to be treated with appropriate caution during this risky escape. One mistake could have jeopardized the whole undertaking, not to mention a loss of life.

Especially during the winter, to move on foot became a challenge and be less likely interrupted by a possible control; as everywhere around the country, life had more or less come to a standstill.

From the start of his escape, Michael took the direction towards the south. He hoped to be able to escape the brutal Siberian cold this way. The settlements, small towns on the way, their names Michael didn't want to remember. He had only to advance farther on his mind.

After winter, springtime always returned and after it, summer. This view carried hope, which was an important help for Michael to overcome, with some relief the pressing difficulties.

It didn't take long for Michael to learn from his encounters with people, even as little as it might have been, and to gain special knowledge from people in special circumstances. Caution was and will be the mother of all wisdom, as well as, you are treated as you treat others.

Beside all this, Michael was not spared hard lessons. He had to understand that to get away on foot from the camp, under the worst possible conditions during a Siberian winter, took time, no matter how hard Michael tried to gain distance from it. He had to find ways to somehow move quicker farther away.

Meanwhile in the camp, it was no doubt and obvious that one camp bed remained empty. Alarm bells were not ringing straightaway; however, it must have become obvious with time that something had happened, and according to rules, an official investigation had to follow immediately to ensure no conspiracy had taken a foothold in the prisoners' camp.

What else could have been done, Michael questioned himself in earnest. The second day and the second night led Michael to an isolated farmhouse again. His modest appearance was, again, well received. This time around, there were no two cows, but Michael still could offer his help where it was most needed.

The question here would be: How could animosities take off at all? Far away in Leningrad of that time and in Moskva, hostile plans were made regardless of their impact on citizens who had no other choice than to remain silent. Most of all it was Stalin oppressing his own people with brutal force. The "guinea pig" communism was declared the holy cow. "The Tsar is far away" had always been a dilemma of Russian history. This didn't only create inequality but also the impossibility to listen better to people's demands. This was also the situation in which Michael found himself during his escape.

No matter how hopeless a situation appeared to be, Michael didn't give up to see the light of hope at the end of his tunnel. The snow already lay heavily for quite some time over the whole country. It slowed Michael considerably in his efforts to gain more distance from the prisoners' camp. Somehow, it appeared, at his second stopover, that peasants united around a table with a hot soup understood each other enough even without words, especially when the shoe pinched the guest.

From the early days with the farmer's family, waiting in a shed was a pair of skis . Without questioning, the skis with two poles found a new owner with Michael. Both sides were happy about it, for it was what was best. Michael expressed his gratitude as best as he could towards such a helping hand.

Reasonably recovered with renewed courage, Michael got on his way again at night; however, this time with much more promising skis. At the farewell, Michael asked the friendly host for his address details. He promised, when time will allow, he would connect back with a letter from home and express his gratitude again towards the kind help he received. The Siberian peasant unexpectedly gave the address of a neighbor who Michael could reach with the skis in a good day's effort.

Michael appreciated this kindness to have a new address to go.

The skis easily glided over the harsh white snow surface. No more deep foot prints that hindered the progress. Suddenly, everything now appeared in a more promising light, and luck found its way back to Michael again.

In almost complete darkness of the night, only partially illuminated from the reflection of the snow surface's white glimmer, Michael continued with his escape. The cold absorbed him so much that he could hardly think about anything else but to keep moving fast. Michael knew well enough what could have happened if somebody, out of the blue, would have recognized the fugitive. Another escape could have been very unlikely because during war times different rules apply.

Although Michael couldn't use his strength to full capacity anymore, the skis moved him surprisingly so quickly to the new destination of the peasant whose address was given to him earlier. In this endless Siberian landscape, telephones were not yet existing.

Although no news of a potential visitor had reached the address, Michael was welcomed, especially when the host let Michael understand that he was to put his skis outside against the house wall, come inside, and leave the cold out.

A belief in the good of some humans found there, at least for a moment, a new anchor. At the end of that day, more precisely the escape during another dark night, Michael still experienced new challenges and told himself that he was now on his way to an escape for some time. Peasants, especially, have, through a closer contact with the Mother Nature, a better understanding where real help is needed.

Therefore, it happened that the other peasant didn't hesitate to invite Michael to come into the house, adding that the terrible cold is not good for anybody.

A communication remained difficult because Michael had no time to learn the Russian language. Here in Siberia at that time, Russian language was the only one commonly used. But it is also said, "Where is a will, there's always a way." And so, it turned out true also this time.

The Siberian peasant knew well enough that the sufferers were not the ones to blame for their fate.

On the first day of Michael on skis, he got away farther than on foot, an estimated twenty kilometers. Before he had to struggle with masses of snow to get through on foot. But with the skis, there were only minor hurdles.

The stopover on the third day, at a Siberian peasant's home, went without incident. Where the modesty and consideration found a common ground on either side, words were not really needed to find out where "the shoe pinched" somebody like Michael.

Hunger was most dominant because an empty stomach could not deliver the much needed warmth for a body. This emptiness of the stomach wasn't to be the only concern.

Hunger could, however, not only be held responsible when winning a goal was the principal objective. How to keep hunger in check became only one of the many tasks to survive. The task to keep oneself clean in such cold snowy weather without being asked and, on top of all that, in sparse daylight during the winter time . At least in one sense, the cold contributed to lessen sweating.

Otherwise, it was the strong memory of home and the family that essentially helped to build the necessary bridges to overcome difficulties. At this very moment, the question also arose: Who could possibly handle all this?

After day three, day four also arrived. Until that day, Michael experienced mainly good people—peasants who had nothing on their minds other than straight openness with a natural view towards humanity.

Not to become a burden to others, Michael put on his skis again late at night. It was important for him to remain undetected, especially from the officials side who he had little to no idea how to deal with in the Russian language.

The severe cold persisted from day three to four. The resting time with food replenishment helped him to regain some much-needed confidence to tackle the almost unimaginable still remaining four thousand kilometers back home to Transylvania. From the beginning, the skis helped Michael gain more distance. From the weather, he also received a helping hand: No new snow fell out of the sky.

People brought to the brink of the possible, often is then decisive what subconsciously with hope have become available in everybody's life. This can turn out into a David-Goliath fight, where David becomes the head and Goliath the body. They both have to cooperate; otherwise, there will be no winner. So much, so little with regard to the demands of a survival situation.

While moving on skis, Michael's mind naturally joined in its rhythm. In the meantime, springtime had wishfully come closer. The hope in this situation supported so much that other possibilities than to escape on skis might have occurred only by chance. With the existing winning situation with a pair of skis, Michael didn't want to risk under any circumstance, especially in the middle of an unforgiving cold winter.

One of the only options he had on his mind was to progress as a blind passenger, hopefully on a train or even as a hitchhiker as soon as Michael came closer to more populated areas. Michael wanted to provoke his luck as war bells of the Second World War could be heard even from afar.

To always have luck on your side was asking for too much, no matter what circumstances Michael was in. The following dawn, already almost exhausted from the night's march even on skis, a farmer's building appeared when a resting time was urgently needed. This time, however, no luck for Michael. On the contrary, he faced a rebuke straight away. "What is going on? We don't welcome hobos. Go to hell," he was told. A bitter disappointment for Michael. What to do now in this situation? Well, there was only one thing left for Michael: To keep trying his luck. At least the dog on the property didn't respond the same way. He approached Michael silently, sniffing his legs. All this wasn't enough for the other peasant to change his mind.

In such a desperate situation, good advice was hard to come by for Michael. Hesitating would have only added to the problems. Therefore, Michael decided to continue on his skis. Luck, however, had not yet abandoned Michael completely. It was still on his side. Luck just accidentally took another turn in Michael's direction, which unexpectedly brought him to another, not too far away, farm house.

12

PAYSANS STICK TOGETHER

Again, a dog was the first one to welcome Michael. He went around Michael, recognizing, in his understanding, that a good person had arrived. Wagging its tail, the dog went back to the farmhouse to pass the good news on. The farmer appeared first from a distance then came his wife. They must have realized from the situation that Michael was somebody who was in need of an urgent help as they couldn't miss the marks of Michael's poor condition. Michael was invited with open arms to come into the much warmer house.

No questions were asked. A chair in front of a table, where he could sit down in the well heated lunchroom of the farmhouse, was offered to Michael. The skis remained outside, leaning against the house wall.

The minor daily necessities received a real lift. Michael was allowed to use a bowl filled with water, soap, and a towel to do the necessary cleaning of himself. Michel's feet, at last, enjoyed the freedom of getting rid of the heavy shoes and the thick woolen socks. The host on the other side showed only satisfaction, accompanied by friendly gestures. Whether the other side had an idea that they accommodated a prisoner of war or not was no problem for the couple. They knew too well that people could often get into trouble without reasonable explanations. The thought crossed their minds: *Why have we all this trouble on the earth?*

Aren't we all humans and have no right to make life more difficult than it is, especially for others?

Besides the couple, another voice, namely that of a child, could also be heard from the room next door. In the first instant, Michael became frozen with shock because back at home a new born child must have waited for him during his absence as a prisoner of war. Was it a boy or a girl? How was his wife doing? Was everybody alive and reasonably in a good health?

Michael got his composure back quickly, covering up his fears from an uncertainty by showing his joy for children saying that the couple is blessed with a child and that may the God Almighty remain with all of them. Michael wanted to see the grandchild also for himself, welcoming it with his own few words of: Beautiful, lovely child, you are the joy for everybody.

All barriers disappeared. A young life managed to overcome the unfortunate so often common thoughts expressed over human relations. No wonder that even this short stay of Michael gave him new energy to continue his way to escape home. Michael's well-being also helped him to face the challenges of a new day.

The farther Michael managed to get away from the war prisoners' camp, the more he tried to include hours during the day for his escape. The days of January and February were still very dark, while the snow only reflected minimal daylight. The bitter cold remained constant. It remained so cold that it couldn't snow anymore. One had to stay active in the open if one wanted to remain alive. The face and nose required particular special attention so as not to turn bluish from chilblains. The best control over it would have been the watchful eyes of a companion and to keep a watchful eye on each other. As this was not possible, Michael was left on his own with this task. The hand had to, therefore, come out of the mittens regularly in order to feel very quickly whether or not the nose and face still felt something. In case of even any doubt, there was only one recipe to address the problem: Grab snow and rub the area intensely to bring the face and nose back to life. Meanwhile, the ears found themselves well protected under a fur hat; the same happened to the hands in the fur mittens.

Solid leather boots protected the feet, going half way up the legs which the trousers narrowly covered on top to keep snow out from the boots. As a protection, Michael could only close his eyes if necessary.

Back on his skis in the snow fields, Michael didn't miss to pay special attention to the environment and its changes. Bluish-green aurora northern lights appeared also during the day like stripes of flames over the horizon. This helped to supply some light that indicated that the northern permafrost area hadn't gained enough distance yet from Michael's move. In some places, summer had managed to already open up frozen surface. It was here that first low fir trees showed up. They remained small, not gaining any height.

Michael couldn't have made more observations. The goal to be back at home one day still lay too far away. The fear of being recognized by the wrong people constantly followed him. Despite that, Michael became only more determined to continue.

During his last stay on a farmhouse, Michael gained confidence with the new address that was given to him. Even when this address was farther away, he still determined to give this "tough nut a crack" too.

This time, the hours during the day had to also serve Michael's advance. He didn't encounter a single person on his way. This, at least, became a small consolation for the bitter winter cold. It was also the main reason to risk an escape from the prisoners' camp during winter only. The price for such an undertaking was also without a doubt stressful. Resting in this incredible cold was no option under any circumstances. What help was available for Michael to keep him going? To distract himself from all these demands he had chosen, Michael counted up to a hundred every forward pass with his right ski first and then with the left ski each time.

This kind of distraction helped Michael reach his day's target just before complete night fall.

If and how this message of an arrival at this next address made it in advance didn't bother Michael too much. As a matter of fact, a dog again took first notice of Michael when he approached the farmhouse. There was no treat for the dog this time around; instead, a gentle touch with the hand over the dog's head would be enough.

Already mentioned, the previous farmer was kind enough to open another door for Michael. How this came to happen remained a secret with the stars. The fact was that Michael, the escapee, appeared exhausted to the extent that he hardly could remain on his legs. He could neither talk nor answer questions. He was again fortunate that the world still had good people. So, it had become immediately evident that somebody had simply arrived who was in urgent need of help—a reminder that nobody was here to be blamed for a war. Other higher ranking people had the courage to carry all the responsibilities on their shoulders for the unlimited trouble caused by war. An explanation with words was always quickly on hand, for instance: The "lower society" had to carry the burden of what the "responsibility carriers" had on their minds. A justification for a power grab finds an end when it comes to put a bill on the table.

Bill or not, Michael had to come to terms with his "own bill," for there was nobody else to whom he could have handed it over. For Michael, it turned out so much better that there were still people who could help each other when help was required. In Michael's case, it turned out that he was offered a bed to lie down straightaway to regain some strength.

Michael couldn't believe that he had fallen asleep immediately when he woke up after a few hours woke up. Nobody in the house had something to say about it; on the contrary, it was the dog who announced that the visitor had woken up.

Meanwhile, the night outside had changed into complete darkness. Although Michael felt recovered and much better, it was too early, at least for the moment, to continue with his escape. Hope, which allowed him a glimpse of freedom, became the driving force for Michael.

The evening then went on in a friendly, assisting atmosphere ; although, communication in the Russian language didn't go easily. Wasn't this enough proof that when humanity was at home, no words were needed?

At the same table, Michael had dinner with the farmer-couple. It remained important for Michael to receive something warm in his stomach, as he was out in the cold too much. Michael had to eat very slowly and carefully not to unnecessarily upset his stomach. He also realized the farmer-couple fully understood. As a grateful gesture, Michael gave a helping hand with the clean-up in the kitchen. This came as a surprise to the farmer's wife to watch a stranger who did her job in the kitchen so well.

In the years of the early 1940s, television wasn't yet known in many parts of Siberia. This then became a good reason not to spend time in front of a TV. Michael needed not to be asked whether or not he was tired enough to go to bed. As soon as he disappeared under the blankets of the bed that was specially prepared for him, his eyes could only turn over shortly before they shut down for a good night's deep sleep.

It had been, by then, a long time since Michael experienced such a good and uninterrupted night's sleep. The next morning, however, he couldn't say that he had slept enough. A reminder of a good sleep's remained in his eyes, which his hands tried to rub out. It gave him, at least for a moment, a feeling to have become even more tired. This couldn't be helpful to anybody; a new day and as a guest of a farmer couple demanded renewed efforts.

At that time during winter, work was only scarcely available, even on a farm property. Michael found out quickly that the farmer kept himself busy inside the house by lining the inside walls with wooden planks to create a better insulation against the cold outside. The planks had arrived by rail from far farther south. Almost nobody owned a car there at the time. During the long-lasting cold winter, no motor wanted to spring into action. If somebody owned a motor vehicle, it was advisable to shut it down and protect it against the severe cold for up to six months during the winter season.

Michael liked this timber, which invited him to put his hands on it, too. The host could only agree to it because more than two all-around skilled farmer's hands could do much more and, on top of it, much better. A bit of a feeling of home took hold of Michael. The two peasants worked nicely together. Already the smell of timber reminded Michael of his small workshop, adjacent to his house. A hand saw cut the nicely planed timber planks to the required length then were joined together. Small pin nails fixed the planks to the wall frame. The farmer filled the empty spaces in between with wool from the sheep. A better insulation was not even to think off. This added a lift to the beauty of the interior of a room, as well as a practical good insulation against the unforgiving bitter winter's cold.

The work went ahead well because both farmers knew what to do and did not stand in each other's way. The pin nails also found their right application without leaving hammer marks on the timber's surface or bluish marks on the fingers from the hammer.

"Well done so far! We've earned a small dinner with a coffee too. Did you hear me Sarah?"

Hearing the name of his wife, a cold shiver ran down his spine. "What a coincidence! My wife also has the name, Sara. This is a sad story. I better leave it alone. I'm prevented from being with her anyway. The birth of our second child must have gone well with God's help. From here on, I'm getting only more impatient to return home. By the way, how does your wife spell her name, Sara? With or without an H at the end?" Michael inquired.

"Here she is, she can tell you best how she writes her name."

"My name is simply written with an H at the end," the farmer's wife replied.

"This means that our wives differ already by their names. My wife's name is written without an H at the end of her name. This doesn't mean, however, that we do not equally like our wives." Michael said.

"So far, we've worked well together. Words wouldn't help even a good thirst nor a hunger and, not to mention a, much needed warmth," responded the host.

"When we talk about family, you have, at your advanced age, left behind much of the work with your children."

"You are right when we talk about work. Our two sons have moved far away into town because they have the idea of a better life there. It comes always to one and the same: We wreck ourselves first as much as we can and find out only much later that something has gone missing in our lives. While we are going to eat and also have coffee, we should find out what else is on our minds. Sarah, we are ready. How far have you come in your kitchen?"

"You've only to take a seat at the table. Make sure your hands are clean and off we can go."

The wall that divides people too often has also been opened without much talk. After a midday break with a luncheon, all work on the two remaining walls went smoothly. Then still before the night's complete darkness, the wooden strips on the floor and the ceiling were mounted through a miter joint in the corners.

After dinner together in the evening, the host declared, "We are going to put a bed now in the new room where our guest can sleep well enough tonight."

The kindness experienced there, Michael didn't want to unduly extend. Therefore, before going to bed in the new room, Michael indicated that he wanted to leave again as early as possible next morning. During his stay, he regained sufficient confidence to move on but didn't want to disrupt the hosts' night sleep. It was only by coincidence that he picked up the name of the farmer's wife. Otherwise, no other name was mentioned because nobody there had an interest to uncover that a prisoner of war was seeking refuge. This again showed how official and unofficial sides can work apart from each other even during a war time. The Siberian peasant knew quite well that not all people are bad like the way politics can possibly make them.

Before leaving, Michael received a connection of address of friends. This time, however, some farther away than in the previous days and nights' walk.

He got out of the bed when it was still dark, feeling much recovered from the previous hike. To Michael's surprise, the farmer couple also got up from their warm beds to bid him farewell. The pair of skis with the two poles were still leaning against the house wall.

Outside, without the protection of a house, the bitter cold of the Siberian winter welcomed everybody. The sky stretched with only little light across wide, white snow fields that gentle hills interrupted the almost never ending flat Siberian landscape.

The snow covered the land for quite some time, sparkling ice crystals covered far and wide the surface that supported an easy and fast gliding of the skis. This promised to give Michael a good advance for the day from the start.

The month of January was introduced, not like at home in Kleinschelken, by a bell-ringing from the church fortress. An increase in the severity of the winter cold in the beginning of the first months of the new year somehow indicated where time had arrived in the year. No wonder that Michael could only ponder on how to crack the difficulties of an advance under such severe winter conditions. However, each move with one ski after the other strengthened the hope of reaching his home again. Michael had to get accustomed to keeping his mouth shut and gritting his teeth to stop the cold from entering his head and chest too easily. Michael's thoughts were however everything else but held on ice . More than ever before, his memories returned strongly. They preoccupied Michael so much that he created a bridging to look further with his iron will for the almost unsurmountable difficulties.

It had to be extremely cold because not even a wolf nor fox, let alone a hare came across Michael's way. Contrary to Michael, those creatures were hiding in snow caves, retreating in hibernation as nature completely lacked in food. Nevertheless, Michael didn't miss out on regular short breaks. The nose was more in demand than the mouth, where the retained air escaped only in a small vapor into the open. In the pockets of his fur jacket from the prisoners' camp, Michael was holding back some pieces of bread. His stomach could estimate, almost with a watch's accuracy, when it was time for another piece of bread. To do so, Michael had to stop his move on the skis for a short time so that the outside cold could not overcome the body's efforts for warmth.

All this distraction helped the time to pass quicker. There wasn't much to see anyway. A white glimmer of snow covered the land as far as the eye could see. The sky couldn't tell that during the year were also times when the sky shined in a deep blue color. During the day, the sky was shrouded in gray color and at night almost in a complete black as long as the stars could send their lights, unless clouds prevented it.

Michael kept checking his direction regularly. How far the railway line was running parallel to his path. He avoided coming too close to the railway line because his memories of the train transport to the prisoners' camp were still too fresh. Michael didn't want anybody to become aware of him while he was escaping.

The railway line started to preoccupy Michael. How he could possibly return home with it. He also realized that, in the long term, the many little distances he only could manage on foot will become, sooner rather than later, too stressful therefore slowing down only his homecoming. The idea of a "blind train passenger" didn't leave him anymore. The direction had to be maintained, of course, to the southwest, away from Siberia.

Michael still had the next farmer's address that he received from his last visit. The explanation on a piece of paper helped him to almost stumble across it.

A lean time of hunger and tiredness didn't wait to show up. During harsh winter times, local people were accustomed to collect the bark from the only small existing forests. They went through with a hand driven mincer, which supplied a flour substitute when properly prepared. This replaced the well and truly better known loaf of bread. The main thing remained, the stomach received something to work on, even if it was short-lived. For Michael, the most important thing was to keep moving.

The next stopover showed up in the wide, open flat countryside. Another timber farmhouse that was painted outside with a reddish colour with a dark green roof clearly stuck out in this icy winter desert.

It also seemed that a dog was watching over these rural properties. The dog was the first to announce the arrival of Michael, barking this time. He must have known that everything was all right. Michael took the skis off first, when he arrived in front of the house, saying to himself, *Oh what a relief!*

Then the other farmer appeared a few moments later from the house into the open. The door was straight away shut behind him because the cold outside was not welcome in the warmer house.

To the farmer, Michael responded as best as he could with his limited knowledge of Russian. The paper with the plan on how to get there and the few written notes on it helped the stay outside in the cold to be as short as possible.

"Come into our warm house, please," the farmer invited.

Michael understood without difficulty. The skis with the poles remained outside, leaning against the house wall again.

This time Michael heard the voice of a child when he entered the house's living area. To connect with memories was not easy for Michael at all because it was impossible for him to know exactly about the fate of his wife and their newborn second child. However, without hesitation, Michael had a ready smile, gently caressing the child's arms in the cot. No words were needed. With this gesture, the elderly couple with the young couple gained immediate mutual confidence in Michael, something that a gesture to a little child could only achieve.

It was interesting that no questions were asked; nobody was curious why Michael had chosen such difficult conditions for his excursion. During the war, everybody who lived far away from the battlefields in the west was happy enough not to become involved in such nonsense. Therefore, questions made no sense. Although Michael was very tired, he didn't want to have unnecessary attention on himself. That's why he also offered a helping hand to them. After the dinner, it was more than welcome that somebody else would help clean the kitchen. Michael didn't mind giving a helping hand as he most likely was the hungriest one in the house. The saying, *Never look a gift horse in the mouth*, also held a significance here. Therefore, everything warm, which could satisfy a hungry stomach, was also more than welcome for Michael. Again, no questions were asked and what was put on the table was accepted because real hunger is always the best cook. Apart from this, the hot soup, accompanied by the silence, with its dumplings and some meat was well received by everybody.

The nature dictated a daily order to everyone as the bitterly winter cold left more or less room for experiments. To hold firmly together made sense especially in the family, could Michael experience also with a family of a Siberian peasant.

In the back of Michael's head, the idea of a "blind passenger" on a train didn't want to leave him. Such a journey had to go only in the direction of his home still far, far away in the south/west. Only this way, Michael could see the possibility of an escape from all these uncertainties without forgetting the inhumane demands.

Back to the visit to the latest Siberian farmer: There was no problem to give each other a helping hand because more hands could simply do more than only one hand.

Far away in the west, the Second World War hadn't yet stopped. Here in faraway Siberia, not even news about the war reached people in the area. Nature already took enough care with its own elements. There was no need for humans to contribute something else. The constant demand to survive was already sufficient enough to keep everybody busy.

No questions were asked when Michael received the luxury of a bed entirely for himself. He was, however, not entirely alone because he shared the room with the baby in its cot. Neither one disrupted the night's sleep of the other, while they both had enough reason to sleep well. Sleeping in a warm bed was the best medicine against the menacing cold from outdoors for everybody. Nobody had to be either educated or told about this. Nature already demanded this kind of discipline.

This night passed quietly and quickly too. Michael gave his best adjusting to this family life. Only upon request, he followed what the others did. This way Michael overcame the language barrier. Where there was a will, there was also a way here.

Michael repeatedly reminded himself that his main target was to move with his escape. Therefore, to bid farewell to this warm and friendly place could not wait any longer. The farmer's family had a good idea why Michael found himself in a difficult situation, and this didn't happen because of his fault. There was also no question when it came to support Michael with at least some provisions. They understood well the situation Michael found himself in, which could have happened to anybody. The nature of Siberia already taught people modesty in life and why help could only be available limitedly. Even the famer's family depended much on the railway transport of goods because very little could only be grown during the short summer season.

To continue his escape, Michael still had no other choice than to use his skis. On his farewell, Michael was surprised when he received a big hug from the famer's family who had shown compassion, even towards a stranger.

The dog didn't hesitate to accompany Michael for a short distance. Another address for a good day's marching distance was also handed to Michael. This time, it was not the address of a farmer because farmhouses were only scattered across the wide, open land. Life had so far never been easy here. Even food for animals had to be brought in by the railway from far and wide as long as the weather conditions allowed it to happen.

A train had, usually in winter, a wide shovel to the front of its locomotive engine, going across the railway lines. When on full steam ahead, the shovel pushed the snow up and into both sides of the railway lines like a snowstorm that hurriedly escaped on both sides of the train into the air.

Only at temperatures colder than negative forty degree Celsius, a train remained in its depot. When this happened, the life in Siberia became extraordinary difficult, because almost everything went missing and came to a halt.

At Michael's departure of that day, it remained still bitterly cold. Snow had been around for quite some time already, packed firmly on the surface with a dirty gray dirty color. It was too cold to snow. On this day, Michael turned on his skis towards the suspected railway line. He would have liked to know about the existing time table that goes towards the direction of his home. All he had to do was to find about it himself.

FINDING THE RAILWAY LINE AGAIN

Michael frequently visited the railway embankment along the countryside, but only for short moments, to find out if the snow on the railway lines had not disappeared with a recently passing train. The direction of the train could also be determined by which side of the rail sleepers the snow had accumulated. No snow on the rail lines showed that a short while ago a train had passed. Only time could deliver to Michael a useful answer. For the time being, to fulfil the day's target was most important for Michael.

It was already mentioned that the day's target was not a farmer's house for a change. Michael was anxious to see what would turn up this time. The anxiety could not be helpful this time around. Still before darkness, Michael experienced a surprise when, for the first time during his escape, he arrived in a small village with only a small number of houses spread around. The houses didn't have the look of a farmhouse. Windows with their shutters and a few visible doors gave the impression that there was no room for animals or farm materials. Michael could do nothing but ask himself: How will I be able to get along with this new situation?

He didn't choose the first house for a stopover. Although the darkness had already fallen, Michael chose almost blindly one of the nearest houses. No dog was there for a change. Shutters from one window allowed dim light to shine through. The moment Michael knocked on the front door, more light appeared in the house. Who rides late in the night with the wind? Could it be the Heaven's child? What came to Michael's mind and if the house occupants had similar thoughts?

As a matter of fact, Michael was rather exhausted from the day's excursion. Therefore, more thoughts of this kind would preoccupy him. What kind of reception might he face? Subconsciously, he told himself, *You are treated as you treat others.*

Michael's expectations lived up to what he wanted. However, questions about such an unexpected visit couldn't be avoided. What should the other side think about it? Only the humanity could connect to such obvious difficulties. As a matter of fact, the house owner invited Michael without hesitation in the Russian language, "Please come into our house. Nobody will last long in this cold outside." The host's additional gesture with his hand directed him into the house, which was also understood without words.

Everybody knew that nobody was to blame for the far away battles of the World War II. People were mostly drawn into a conflict without being involved in it.

Only the poor appearance of Michael, after so many challenges, said it all. After another demanding day of escaping in reduced daylight and in a complete darkness in the evening, there was nothing more left to talk about. This was evident too for every human being, no matter where he/she was living. The invitation into the house was followed by encouragements like: Take off your heavy winter clothes and then wash yourself in our bathroom. There is still from our dinner also something left for you. Unfortunately, we can't offer you your own bed for the night but a mattress on the floor with a blanket in the entrance hall will certainly still be sufficient, so the warmth of the house will stay also with you. As you can see, we haven't got much, but are more than happy to share it with you.

It didn't take long for Michael to fall deeply asleep as soon as he lay down on the mattress. The following night followed in complete silence. It was the host's family that called in the morning to get out of the bed.

Outside the house darkness still reigned. People there had to work for their living. Much of a choice was never given. Everything that could support life was welcome. Michael could at least rub his eyes awake first. He didn't want to appear out of step with that family's life by remaining on his mattress as long as needed. On top of this, Michael would have been in the way when the family moved from one room to another one.

To start the day, a bowl full of water already waited for Michael so he could clean the night's sleep away. The family of the host couple, including the young son and his wife had already started breakfast in the living room when Michael joined them. He hesitated but was determined when he was invited with a hand sign to take a seat with them.

However, Michael couldn't help himself but think how could he carry on with his escape and not become a burden for the others. In his opinion, these helpful others didn't deserve to share Michael's misfortune. Who had the answer for it, once been caught by misfortune? Straight after breakfast, Michael couldn't wait any longer to start the new day. The host reminded Michael, "There is no need to be in a hurry so early in the morning. It's still bitterly cold outside. Don't get mixed up, neither with hurry nor with while. As we follow our daily routine, mainly with work, you are welcome to rest a bit longer because you will need it. I'm also sure you won't set our home ablaze. You don't look like somebody who is capable of doing this."

Only a trace of a smile on his face, Michael responded, "I'm grateful for the confidence I receive from you. Time will tell and be also helpful." After that exchange, not much was said, but it was enough to understand each other.

To extend his stay for another day appeared also for Michael a good idea. Time allowed him then to think over the possibilities he had to change his escape for a better one. Not to be in the host's way, Michael watched carefully where he could step in with a helping hand. In a household of five people, including Michael, help was always welcome, especially when the Siberian winter leaves everybody inside the house.

In winter was the time to prepare indoors, what was needed and outside during the spring and summer time. Here in Siberia, spring and summer were only short-lived but much more characteristic with longer balmy summer days, much depending on the northern geographical position where the sun was shining all day throughout the night, especially during the months of June and July. Nature also showed in Siberia it's much more friendly face.

At the moment, it didn't happen yet because the winter still asked for its attention. Therefore, it didn't take long during the day that the dark night hours again had taken over. Michael still had a good idea from the evening before how to fit into the family's life, of course through a helping hand.

After dinner together at one and the same table, Michael explained to the hosts that he wanted to go to sleep early, so that he could start to continue his tour early the following day.

After Michael said this, it didn't take long to happen. Without a word, the housewife had prepared breakfast especially for Michael on the table. He knew how to appreciate this kindness which he expressed with a hug. What next? The answer was with Michael! Michael put the pair of skis on both his legs, holding the ski straps in his hands which had, at their pointed end, disc rings mounted to prevent the poles from sinking into the snow.

His plan to continue the escape with the railway came now one step closer as he made a shortcut first straight into the direction of the local railway line. Slightly elevated, the railway line stuck out visibly in the outskirts of the little town. Michael really didn't expect to see the train when he arrived there.

What he didn't fail to do was to investigate with the railway official at the local station when the next train to the south would be due. So much Michael could understand that the train was expected tonight. The joy over these good news Michael had to keep to himself because that "egg" had still to be delivered. The next question was: How could Michael spend his waiting time best?

Michael had no intention to return to his last accommodation in the village out of respect. What a choice he had other than move outside the village center not to attract unnecessary attention and watch the village life from a distance. Michael had his plan ready to do his next move with the train. How was it going to happen, remained to be seen.

HOW TO GET ON THE TRAIN

Still before complete darkness, the scheduled train arrived at the local station. It was a freight train. Only a few passenger compartments were connected to it, this time running into the southern direction. If Michael wanted to grab this opportunity for a further escape, he was well advised to act fast. He waited on the opposite side of the station; first, a few steps away from the train carriages, so he could remain more anonymous. He was lucky that one of the passenger compartments had stopped right in front of him. Not even one passenger could be seen on the platform or in the compartment. Michael hurried to open the last back door. He closed it and so became a passenger on a train, his skis included.

To remain hidden, Michael opened, right in the back of the carriage, a door leading into a small compartment of its own. The purpose of this room must have been for a control person in the case of a prisoners-of-war transport. It was located in the back of the driving direction to minimize the cold coming from outside. What difference it made for Michael, not to be officially on a train as a prisoner of war! Finally, this train also gradually started, pushing one carriage after the other until a uniformed movement of the whole train was achieved.

Michael felt this like a new experience. It meant, however, to remain watchful, not be detected as an illegal passenger. Therefore, Michael did not shut his little compartment door, so he could find out what was going on in the other parts of the train.

Michael watched carefully from a simple timber bench whether a ticket controller appeared in the other compartments or not. The time could, meanwhile, tell Michael that no control was needed as no other passenger was on the train.

Besides the passenger carriages, most of the other carriages were loaded with goods. Places along this railway line received the goods they needed across the vast Siberian territory.

The train, with this longer steam locomotive, kept going with coal fire, which most likely originated from one of the prisoners' camps. Michael felt more freedom as a stowaway train passenger.

Entirely without problems could this "experiment" remain. The more hours on the train passed, more tiredness got hold of Michael, not to mention how the stomach felt. Slowly but surely, the cold couldn't be stopped to creep into the train compartment. At least on the first day of this train journey, Michael already gained considerably more distance than he could have done on foot and later on his skis the previous days. The rule of one step at the time remained to keep the rush out when he wanted to succeed .

The hunger and tiredness couldn't, however, be easily ignored, even with the new conditions on a train. Self-distraction again became the answer for Michael, at least for the time being; and for a distraction, nothing was closer than to look simply out of the side window. It's smaller size in Michael's compartment could still tell him what Siberia was like.

After the time on the train, the region slowly changed from an endless flat white country up to the horizon, first to gentle hillsides where slowly the nature introduced traces of the green vegetation. Further south, conifers slowly gained a foothold in small forests. Their dark green needle-dress was welcoming to the eyes like a resting place. Where the snow was receding, brown yellow grass patches showed through. When in the summer, green took over.

While Michael's eyes rested in these pictures, his body retreated into the tiredness. He had to stay alert and not fall asleep. This was the demand, and Michael had no other choice when he wanted to go home again. At the few stations on the way, Michael was hiding under one of the benches so as not to be spotted by somebody.

Every now and then, after some travelling time, the steam engine received water at a station into its steam tank and coal to its furnace.

Where this coal had originated from remained everybody's guess. Water especially could have become a problem because of the icy temperature outside. For that reason, water was better to be stored in closed underground tanks, avoiding it from getting solidly frozen.

Michael knew he could not stay on the train forever without something to eat. When he had to use a toilet, the one in his compartment near his hiding place was close and good enough. Simply behind that door in the back of the carriage, one could see a wooden bench with a hole which was covered. No flushing was required, because the railway line was visible underneath, meaning that in the winter such a visit had to be a short one. A typical toilet smell could, however, not be avoided. One advantage at least came out it, that passengers, if any, were not keen to take a seat close to this location. Michael didn't mind this because he found himself in a more secure area from other possible passengers.

15

NECESSITY OF A DISRUPTION

The problem of hunger and tiredness didn't want to abandon Michael. How could he possibly "kill two birds with one stone"? Already in a complete darkness, Michael decided to leave the train unseen, skis under his arms from the opposite side of one of the railway stations. He was hopeful to secretly leave the train this way. What next? This became the difficult question. As soon as the train left, the life around the station calmed down.

Nobody could be seen anymore. The lights outside were switched off. Michael had to ask himself: What now? After all, the day on the train went well enough. One important fact was: Michael remained undetected. From now on, he had to change his undetected role if he wanted the help from other people. How it could happen or not, remained to be seen.

The reason to put a question mark on this was that Michael couldn't convince himself at the very moment. What would be more demanding for him to continue his escape on the skis or the train? What mattered most at the end was to give it time and don't rush things.

As Michael strolled on foot along the main road with his skis over his shoulder, almost in front of every house a dog's barking announced the stranger. In a more densely populated area, a dog's barking had a different meaning to the one in the wide-open countryside.

From one house came out light, when the house door opened. "Is there still somebody around in the cold outside," came a voice out of the house. The light didn't miss Michael. As soon as the person saw Michael while stepping out, the door was immediately closed behind him, while the voice let to understand, "Who is so crazy to be on foot at night in such a terrible cold?" In the first instant, Michael was not ready for an answer. When the man or maybe a woman had no clue about what was happening outside, he/she returned to the house entrance. Michael picked up his courage and asked once more, of course in the Russian language, "Is here a place to stay overnight?" This kind of a surprise didn't find a response straightaway. A short while later, the Russian house owner found his words and replied, "Have I heard right that there is somebody outside in this terrible cold who needs help? Before you come into my house, you better tell us, who you are and what you have on your mind. You better come into the house, because outside we can't understand each other. To my eyes, you must be a tough sportsman on skis. Not far from us, the temperature dropped yesterday to minus fifty degrees Celsius. Under these conditions a survival becomes questionable."

Michael understood even with his limited knowledge of Russian what the other side was saying. During different situations, he had picked up at least so much of the Russian language, which enabled him of a basic understanding.

Michael also understood that nothing was really lost so far. As his move on the train took place at a right time, he considered himself lucky.

"We have never heard that this time of the year no train was running because of a too cold temperature. You should be able to rely on the train with your excursion."

Michael was quite happy to hear that everybody thought he was a tourist on the train who was seeking, during a stopover, a place where he could stay overnight. In the house, there were also other people. If they were visitors, Michael could have fitted perfectly into this family.

His main concern remained, however, not to be questioned about money for the accommodation. Nevertheless, the house dog stayed close to Michael, making sure they both were fond of each other.

Meanwhile the host continued, "You must come from a different country as we can hear that Russian is not your mother tongue. The time is not going to change to something better because the war still continues relentlessly. We are lucky to be a good distance away from these battle grounds, which have never been good for somebody anyway."

The host continued, "What we all need is something to eat and a good night's sleep. Outside in this cold, I'm sure you would have none of it. To share something with you will do no harm to anyone of us. Come in, and take a seat at our table, so we can take better care of your wellbeing.

We have had already dinner so late in the day. To get something warm into your stomach certainly does not hurt you. We don't mind to keep you company because we don't have often visitors."

Michael told himself, *A time shared together with other four people, including a toddler could only be beneficial for a lonely escapist.* He was mainly preoccupied with eating dinner, no words were, therefore, required. No words were needed yet when the bed announced itself. Michael could have his own bed on a temporary mattress in the corner of one room. It remained no doubt bitterly cold outdoors, but in the house, a blanket was enough to keep himself warm.

The night then continued, quiet and undisturbed. Even the dog understood his task to keep company with the guest, confirming to everybody else that everything was fine as he wagged its tail.

Daylight had already started here earlier. Therefore, it was easier to get out of bed much quicker. Michael was told to use the washing facilities the house had to offer. This included a bowl of water, soap, and a towel for his use.

Michael met finally all the family members at the breakfast table. He could do nothing else but think of how to return the courtesy he had received. The little four-year old boy liked to be with Michael. Nothing else was clearer when the little boy took a seat on Michael's lap, where both experienced fun like on a swing that moved them from left to right and backwards.

Michael's situation reminded him about the time in train where he could find out when the next train was due to depart from there. The host was now under the impression that Michael wanted to continue his journey as a train passenger.

Michael's small vocabulary of Russian words didn't change the situation much. At the local station's counter, he received the message: The train doesn't come back today because nothing works here in a hurry.

From there Michael concluded that he would try again the next morning, and it was best not to be too early because the station master also likes to stay a little longer in bed. Until then, it was a good resting time which wouldn't harm anybody.

During the waiting time, nothing could be done in a hurry. Michael instead fell into another deep slumber, and when the house host returned from the local railway station, *There is no need to rush. We've got enough time as the time table informs us*, thought the host, when he saw that Michael had fallen asleep. "A railway journey during the winter is not exactly fun," mentioned the host to his wife. He was not prepared to include her name, simply because out of fear that an official side could have found out that a foreigner was around here, and somebody else could gain an advantage out of this situation. "We never know when we possibly are caught in an unwanted situation", the host continued to his wife.

When Michael woke up, he could only surprise himself when he asked, "How could it happen that I fell asleep during the daylight in a foreigner's house?" He quickly regained his clear mind and spoke out his morning greetings in the living room next door.

"What would you like first? The good or the bad news? Fortunately, I have only good news for you concerning your next train departure. By the way, let's not forget, there is no hurry! In four days, there will be a train in the afternoon that departs from our station. Until then, we will find something to kill the time."

"What can I add to it? There is nothing else to say but thank you. The question however remains, what can I do in the meantime? The best I can offer is to help where it is needed. I can use both my hands. Because where there is a will, there is always a way."

Such an answer was well received in this home and the response didn't have to wait long, "You help us cut the timber, and split it with the axe, which gets us through the winter. I will show you the shed next to the house where the timber is already waiting for you. When all windows and doors stay shut, the temperature shouldn't be all right for this type of work. I've done it myself for many years already and don't mind receiving a helping hand for a change. Our young generation today is not keen of this type of work. They have different ideas about a better life. It seems to me that you have grown out of this age.

You know already, life can deliver also unwanted surprises, if work is not considered a necessity. Well, this all can be easily understood, but it doesn't help us any further. Are you ready? Let's go over to the shed where the timber is waiting"

Said and it was already done! An oven in the shed waited for the right sizes of timber to deliver warmth there. In my opinion, a worker deserves food too, like an oven. Wooden beam pieces, branches, a bow type saw, and an axe made Michael feel at home because he knew how to get along with them. From time to time, a cup of a hot tea in between the work helped to restore some energy, which the cold took away without being asked.

Before another night fall, Michael had already delivered a lot of work and split timber pieces, nicely stacked up for the tiled stove in the house's centre where the coal briquettes were added, maintaining the necessary warmth during the winter.

The new day passed for Michael again well enough. It's also known that whoever who works, sleeps well, and this happened after dinner at one and the same table to all the house inhabitants. Then, the next morning didn't fail to show up. The cold was, however, still around. Despite that, Michael had no problem to know what to do. The timber in the shed still waited for him. When he was ready to swing the axe over the wooden blocks, the door next to him opened cautiously squeaking, and a man entered saying, "I'm the neighbour and have not missed that somebody, despite the cold, is cutting timber into smaller sizes. Once you've finished, you could continue in my place next door."

Michael could only lift his arms, indicating that he had no say on the matter. "Today it's not easy anymore to find somebody who wants to work, regardless of the weather conditions," responded the neighbour. "There is, however, one thing I want to let you know, work is more than enough around here."

At least this way Michael experienced how to spend his waiting time. Whether it made sense or not, was not the question.

The day, when the train was to arrive late in the afternoon, it came surprisingly quicker than anybody in and around the house could have anticipated. Nervous tension had grown in Michael the more the hours of the day advanced. Will he again succeed with the train? What will the host-family, including other locals, think about his way of a departure on the train? This preoccupied Michael's mind constantly.

He remained, however, strongly determined against all the odds that not much more could have been against him, especially as he succeeded so far until now.

The host showed contentment with the orderly way Michael had stacked up the split fire wood pieces. Warmth for the winter was now secured here. When time for a goodbye had arrived early enough, Michael made the host family understand that he was not important enough to receive a carpet treatment. Contrary to it , the host was more than happy to give Michael, for his way, some provisions of basic food. Everybody could see clearly enough that besides his skis and the heavy warm clothing that protected him from the winter's cold, Michael had not much else with him.

BACK INTO THE TRAIN

Alone at the station, Michael could only guess the time when the train was due to arrive and came indeed to a halt. As soon as Michael saw the train coming, he walked quickly across the railway line on to the opposite side where passengers were usually waiting, as he did previously. Nobody else was waiting for the train, Michael was left on his own. In the middle of the train carriages, where the two passenger compartments were located, Michael opened a door right in the back. Quick as a flash, he was in the train that nobody could become aware of him.

Outside reigned almost complete darkness. From a previous experience, Michael knew well enough how to accommodate himself more securely despite poor light conditions. It more or less looked like as if the cabin at the end of the compartment was already waiting for him. A welcome happened easily, and he had reason enough to feel good in the company of only the host provisions.

He took the seat and left the door slightly open. After that he could easily wait for the train's departure. No rush was needed. News arrived more or less the same way to Michael like to the station master. From there, they spread first into the village and then eventually further. It remained important for Michael that no news about a "blind passenger" on the train could take a foothold.

Finally, one by one the train carriages pushed each other into a constant move with an increasing speed. The steam engine had taken coal and water on sufficiently that enabled the train to travel all day and night, even through the snow.

A shovel mounted across the steam engine's front made the snow fly in high arcs away on both sides. Fast blown-up snowflakes found, even through closed windows, access into the carriages, piling up under the windows into heaps of snow. No passenger would have enjoyed this journey in the middle of winter with snow in the carriages.

Michael's proven side-tracking with his eyes, looking forward, to the left, the right, close the eyes for a moment and when opened again, no surprise, everything was still the same as it was before. Michael's ears, however, remained alert, listening thoroughly through the gap when somebody came into the carriage. For the moment, everything appeared going Michael's way.

Most likely did Michael's thoughts help him not to become silenced from the cold, even in the more protected train compartment. How far is the prisoners' camp by now? I started on foot then continued on skis, a good day on the first train and now more than a day's train journey. Altogether, it must add up to more than one thousand kilometres. This was a part of Michael's thoughts while on the train. The fear that something could have gone wrong, he just ignored. His mind told him that he couldn't have control over everything. Hope became his last resort.

So much luck could happen to Michael only during winter because Siberia, with its outlying districts, was not inviting train passengers, especially during its cold peak winter season. Such an assumption also became an essential part of Michael's overall escape plan. Then after all, it remained to be seen how everything was going to work now.

According to the changes in the environment and the days increasing in sun light, Michael must have come a good distance away from where his escape had started. To gain distance within Siberia also meant the number of small towns to bigger ones increased, while the distances from each other became smaller.

A greater number of people resulted in all this too. For Michael, this meant to pay more attention to people. He was determined to stay on this train as long as possible. For the first time, passengers joined the train at stations that became bigger each time. *When will a control person appear?* crossed Michael's mind. As this hadn't happen so far, he could conclude that the winter's cold had still too much to say here.

Michael also did his best to keep his cool, moving more freely within the passengers' compartments without restricting himself only to the more hidden chamber in the back, testing a bench seat for regular passengers from time to time.

At one station, Michael realized that a control took place only at the station's entrance when leaving the train. A plus for Michael!

How far this train would take Michael remained to be seen. On the way towards the south/west, the area changed noticeably from a flat, wide, open country into higher ground interrupted by valleys. White snow fields persisted, however, almost everywhere. Still inside the train, Michael avoided contact with other passengers for a good reason. He was afraid to be recognized as a foreigner.

The food gift from his last stay gave him the strength to move on. Slices of bread with real butter, the magical daily apple, and a bottle with warm tea—all that made a big difference to the conditions Michael went previously through.

A full day and night travel on the train took him again farther. At one station, a surprise was waiting for him when all the remaining passengers on the train left together. Michael concluded that from there, the train didn't go any farther, but a return tour was certainly not on his mind. As quick as possible, he got out the train from the opposite side of the platform in front of the station to avoid a control.

Some distance away from the railway line, Michael was waiting until another locomotive took the carriages back into the direction where they came from. After that, the peace and quiet ruled at the station and around it.

As soon as the train again had left, calm returned and Michael inspected the station from close by. Michael asked himself, *Where are we now and when will another train continue from here into my direction?*

Nobody was present inside the station anymore. A large map on the wall showed where the marked railway lines went far and wide from there. The first major city, Chelyabinsk, on the foothills of the mighty Ural Mountain ranges showed up on the map farther west. A place by the name of Saratov appeared in the direction of Ukraine. Judging this map, the way to Michael's home in Transylvania (Siebenbürgen) was still far away. It was not the time to give up hope. So far at least 1500 kilometres of seemingly hostile country had been left behind. Only the thought, *If I had known this before, it wouldn't have helped me to get that far.* It was therefore only reasonable to gain new courage and move on. A step farther into the right direction delivered a printed timetable on the wall next to the window of the station master. It was not necessarily him who Michael wanted to see.

Going back to the map on the wall, it was already enough to understand the size of this Russian part. Regardless of what has started, it had to also come to an end.

At present, Michael found himself in the town of Kurgan. Eighty years before today, most towns in all the areas were still very small. Progress couldn't reach all these places, and traffic on the road didn't exist yet. Contrary to that time, the Chinese have taken the initiative to build the Silk Road, which will run also through the entire Russian territory connecting China with Europe. Back in 1941, this would have been only a futuristic vision.

The next bigger town was Chelyabinsk. This will be a new experience for Michael after so much countryside, almost deserted from people. A waiting time spent here in Kurgan couldn't have been helpful because waiting doesn't satisfy a hungry stomach.

17

A NEW DISRUPTION

Michael's skis reminded him how to get there. The station's timetable showed that a train for Chelyabinsk was going to leave from there in two days. How accurate a timetable like this could have been remained an open secret for everybody. Therefore, one's own initiative delivered the only answer.

The outside temperature didn't seem so biting anymore, and the occasional less wind helped reduce the snow as well. "Will I manage the two hundred kilometres to Chelyabinsk on my skies? In two days I should make it," Michael convinced himself. *I better start straight away and see how it goes before the next night fall when the cold returns*, thought Michael.

Back on his skis after the train journey, everything felt, at the least, like a new travel experience. As Michael could only expect, he was alone on his way. The snow covered the street; its course hardly visible. Daylight lasted already longer, and Michael had chosen his direction towards the west where the sun was going down later in the day. During this time of the year, it was almost guaranteed not to meet anybody in the street. This also meant that Michael was, for better or worse, left on his own. In his opinion, he assured himself that he had already enough former exercises. What only mattered now was to gain more distance.

Still before the nightfall, Michael looked around the area, hopefully sighting a farmer's building. And indeed, not far off his track, a small number of farm buildings showed up in the south. This number of buildings looked like more than one farmer had settled here.

Out of previous experience, Michael cautiously approached the area. A dog again signaled, with its barking, that a stranger had arrived. Whether it was a small or a big dog, it noticed straightaway that Michael was fond of animals. The dog went first past the ski sticks before sniffing around Michael's legs. In company of the dog, Michael arrived at the entrance door of the largest timber house.

"Is there somebody? What does he or she want?" A voice coming from inside the house to the outside through a still closed door inquired.

"Good evening," responded Michael as his knowledge of the Russian language was not good enough to say any more confidently.

"Let's have a look who is wishing us a good evening in this cold from outside. Nobody could possibly remain there; come in and show me who you are."

Michael had not much to say. With his skis and poles he looked like a winter sportsman who got lost. That thought went through the other peasant's mind. "We can't have the door open much longer, rather come quickly in and leave the cold outside, so that the door can be closed again. Have you escaped from the war? You don't look really happy. None of us likes a war, the lordship up there can talk easily and send others into the battlefields of their own creations. War or no war, what are you doing in your daily life? Where do you come from and where are you heading?"

"I'm only a peasant, too." This was how much Michael could speak with his Russian knowledge.

"In this case, peasants should know how to get along with each other. We just want to make sure you are not on the enemy side. At present, nobody can be cautious enough. According to your appearance, you haven't had much to eat lately, no wonder during our severe winter."

Sofia, we should have some leftovers from our dinner for the poor bugger. By the way, Sofia is my wife. Please take first a seat at our table after having taken off your bulky clothes. After you are used to our warm house interior, I suppose we better provide you also with a bed, so you can stay overnight. Am I right?"

"I can only say, thank you very much," slipped out of Michael's icy lips. There was no need to say much more. The peasant couple had good enough eyes to recognize that somebody out of their own world was in need of help.

After that, hot milk with bread and butter made a welcome change for Michael. The host didn't miss it, only adding, "The milk comes from our own cows. It's healthy stuff to still hunger. You should also know what the work is like on a farm. I'm so far lucky. My son lives with his family in the timber house next door. We do our best and tackle the daily workload together. Tomorrow morning, after a good night's sleep, you can meet him too. We better hurry now into our beds because another day doesn't wait much longer for us. In the evening, we usually don't stay up for hours, especially during winter."

The farmer's wife must have already made a bed for Michael in a room nearby under one and the same roof, which was heated comfortably by a tiled oven located at the center of the room. Under his warm blanket, Michael fell asleep straightaway.

"The early bird catches the worm," the peasant said not without reason. Work won't let us wait for long. It is the peasant's gold. Exactly at the stroke of a bell, the three cows in the shed next to the house announced the time: six o'clock in the morning. Michael didn't miss it. He got out of the bed himself, looked around where he could find the cows' shed. He didn't have to look around much longer, as everybody else in the house was already busy. Without hesitating, Michael showed that he knew how to milk a cow and, first of all, how to clean the floor around a cow and add fresh saw dust and hay. After that, he began to become familiar with each individual cow.

Nobody had to tell Michael, a kick from a cow's hoof was no good at all. For a beginner on a farm, it is recommended never to approach a cow from behind, but rather, face it from the front and carefully touch the cow's head. Michael knew very well that this applied also for horses.

Back to cows: The right way to approach would be to gently touch the cow's belly with a flat hand, move the hand slowly downwards towards the udders slowly. Don't forget to put a clean shiny bucket on the floor underneath the cow, then at a right height, put a stool closest to the cow's side in a secure distance in case a hoof sharply and quickly kicks the bucket, or you, or both.

Then gently touch the udders sideways with both hands, then pull the teats slowly and steadily downwards while opening and closing the hands slightly, so the milk can flow freely into the bucket directly underneath. The cow will, however, not accept a wrong treatment. A sudden kick with a hoof can then be the answer.

Such help was well received in the farmhouse. Michael had only made himself understood where the milk was going from there. He managed this way without words to find a place to stay overnight. The young farmer's family joined at the breakfast table, a reminder how a helping hand could overcome language barriers and bring people from other nationalities closer. At the table, when everyone was all together not much talk was needed. Michael happily joined the family's custom to hold hands in the beginning. Everybody welcomed milk, either pure in a cup, in tea, or coffee, whereas Michael had chosen porridge with milk. It gave him the proper energy he needed for his way farther.

In this cold winter's air, dry lips unmistakably announced a lack of moisture. The bite of an apple, which was kept in a pocket out of the cold, helped Michael to keep this problem at bay for at least a short while.

Michael's escape in skis had to continue that day. Chelyabinsk became the next destination, the first larger place with all its so-called progress. The family at the farmhouse looked like they had some ideas about the situation in which Michael found himself. To bid farewell to

Michael, everybody stepped out of the house and escorted him a short distance, so that a new day could start well for Michael too.

The day started for Michael as another one on skis. The snow still covered the countryside around in a white blanket. Like the day before, the road disappeared almost in the snow, only giving a vague indication where it was leading to. As it would be only expected, nobody else was on the road. Michael neither anticipated to find another farmhouse before Chelyabinsk. He told his skis to better hurry up before a new nightfall would start. The right advice was handy now, especially as city folk differed much from country people. In cities, people seemed to preoccupy themselves only with their own affairs. The time for others came to a waiting list. Right now, his own considerations couldn't be helpful at all. What still mattered were practical solutions.

18

FIRST ENCOUNTER WITH A TOWN

This time around, Michael found one solution: The lights were still on in a pub. Voices could be heard right to the street and, occasionally, even accordion music, something so much different from what Michael had experienced so far. The skis with the poles Michael left outside against the pub's wall.

After a solid entrance door, he couldn't miss the bar counter directly opposite to it. Many of the small tables around were well attended to by only men, as Michael could see for himself. He spoke to the man behind the bar only a couple of words, which he could express in the Russian language, "Work, food, and a bed, who can offer it?"

"We are certainly not short of work, the expectations, however, are usually a different kettle of fish. Do you want to help me as a waiter in my restaurant? I'm short of staff, especially during late hours. I now show you a room where you can get ready for your first appointment. As far as I can see, you need proper clothing as a waiter. My guests won't look too close at you. Otherwise, to speak Russian doesn't appear to be your strong point. You won't need much talking anyway. Most importantly, you understand to present yourself. Let's wait and see how we go. We can't be on the wrong side. The main thing remains that this helps us both."

Michael was really surprised to hear that he, the peasant from Kleinschelken, was going to present himself as a waiter on the side of Siberia at the foot of the Ural Mountains. Here, necessity became the mother of invention, quicker than anybody would have expected, Michael appeared in a striking light blue suit with a bright red tie. Michael showed up at the bar and waited for his boss's approval.

"The guests will let me know for sure what they want. With my support, you will learn in no time what people want, and with a smile on your face, the servicing will work out too. It will remain, however, important to keep an eye on our guests, so that they don't leave before they have paid. If for instance, somebody turns crazy from vodka, I take care of him and get him out of our restaurant faster than he would believe. Remaining kind won't help in all situations. Sometimes action is also needed. In the kitchen behind us is my wife. When she needs a helping hand, are you prepared to assist her too? Just nod your head, and I know that you agree. Any more questions, you can see me behind the bar at any time. Finally, let me tell you that our guests like to be left alone too. I'm sure I've said enough. Let's start now. You can give us a helping hand, and nothing will prevent us to help you."

Work stopped only in the early hours of the next day after a whole night's work in the restaurant. Many guests had arrived; the noise didn't fail to accompany them. The patron was a happy man. No words were, again, needed. Michael just performed everything he was asked to.

Just then, Michael realized how tired he was, so that he could hardly keep his eyes open. His service was well received. From time to time, a snack in the kitchen waited from the patroness for Michael, which he welcomed happily because every hard worker deserves a refreshment every now and then.

Even a tooth brush, comb, brush, soap and a towel were waiting for him in his room. The bed with a proper blanket was prepared by the patroness to help Michael fall straightaway into a deep sleep.

At dawn, Michael didn't need to get for a change up early and not even to think about to be back on the road. As the work in the restaurant continued into the early morning hours, the new working day didn't start before ten o'clock in the morning.

It must have been ages since Michael had slept so deep and well. When he opened his eyes, at first, he felt more tired than he did when he went to bed. This, however, didn't become a stumbling point, considering that in the restaurant was waiting a new working day for Michael.

In the restaurant, what waited for Michael was a mess of disorderly tables, chairs, leftover glasses, dishes, cutlery for tidying up. It was here where the patroness awaited Michael. The patron on the other hand wasn't around yet.

"For a start you did a good job last night. You were a good help to us. Now, first have a seat here at the kitchen table. What would you like for breakfast, so this new day can become a good one again for all of us?"

"A tea will certainly do no harm. Tea, please," answered Michael, nodding his head to make himself better understood. At the end it was important to get the messages through.

"First have a quiet breakfast. Afterwards, I'd like you to give me a hand to wash the dishes, dry them, put them away where they belong. I show you where all of this is supposed to be. Today is Friday, and we can expect more or less a normal day. Around lunchtime, only a few guests usually turn up. They are seeking our warm restaurant for a hot cup of tea. Later during the day, when most have left work, we can expect busy hours. We are really lucky that you found us because together we manage the workload much better. By the way, tomorrow on Saturday, the rush will already start much earlier in the afternoon. A local accordion player will also attract the attention of many music lovers. Our guests will eat and drink and, on the top of, it they will eventually dance. Watch, how many beautiful young ladies will come to us."

Michael showed his hand the wedding ring on his hand, adding to it, "When it comes to dancing, the patroness should know how grateful I am for the help and support I have received."

However, it was still Friday, and the day went on without any dancing. The patron would also say happily, "Another day, another thank you for your good service, Igor." The news about this good helping hand spread locally like wildfire. Luckily, nobody had any questions about Michael's poor Russian communication skills. The patron couple was more than happy that both sides had received good help.

It didn't mean, however, that Michael could not have left on a short notice. It was a dilemma Michael found himself in. He had to give priority to his recovery from the earlier stressful days and weeks if he wanted to reach his goal to go home again. Nobody learned about Michael's secret plan. He must have also understood well enough that in the end nothing in a life is secure. Therefore, Michael had to find a solution that would serve both sides well. He had considered, from the beginning, to stay at the restaurant for a month at least. The patron was, so far, forthcoming that he paid Michael a daily bonus, besides the free accommodation including catering.

Michael's friendly service was well received from all guests. Despite all this, Michael felt uneasy, keeping his secret to himself. Where was he now more at home, on his escape or in Kleinschelken, his home? One step at the time helped get so far at this point. There was no reason not to continue this way.

Friday, Michael's second day as a waiter, went well and fast because everybody was already used to each other. Saturday, the next day, really surpassed Michael's expectations. He couldn't believe how many people the accordion player attracted to the restaurant. Besides eating and drinking, music was also on that day's program as a center of attention.

The music was not only restricted to the restaurant, even the people from the street could freely join this enjoyment.

The musician held his instrument partly secured between his legs, ensuring that polka rhythm as well as marches and much more reached every corner of the restaurant.

Not as a complete surprise, beautiful local ladies arrived as well, and the opportunities had their saying. Everybody who enjoyed music, dancing, and, occasionally, eating with or without a drink was welcome there in the right place.

Michael was acting like a busy bee. Was it his attractive light blue suit with the bright red tie or more his friendly service? Who might certainly have known? As a matter of fact, both the musician and Michael became the center of attention during the entire evening.

As soon as the accordion player invited everyone to dance, the whole place was up and running with full joy. Even the patron couldn't believe what he saw. This was the first time so many people attended the restaurant at once. How much did Igor, the new waiter, have to do with it?

The patron realized that Michael serviced mainly his guests. He asked the musician to stop his music for a moment so that he could address his guests, "Nobody should only work. Let's call my wife from the kitchen and our new waiter, Igor. They both will show our guests that they can do something else and dance together for us all. Let's start the music again, and you, our guests, give them a huge applause, and clap your hands with the music. Everybody take care. Please drink in moderation without moving tables or chairs, and leave the floor free for the dance to continue."

The patron's words were well received. His wife didn't need another invitation. The patron's wife left her apron in the kitchen, and Michael was already waiting to swing his patroness in his arms, and the accordion music continued without delay, which took everybody back on to the floor.

Michael couldn't believe what kind of a different life he could suddenly experience. His wishes to go back to where he really belonged, Transylvania his home country, remained unchanged.

His fate was still hanging in an uncertain balance. The patron on the other hand must have had different ideas about Michael, his new waiter. Serving two masters at the same time didn't work properly; therefore, the patron and Michael came to this crossroad the longer this cooperation was to last. Michael was well aware that it could not continue forever.

For the time being, it was enough for Michael to have a break from the previous stressful uncertainties. Only the end would show Michael, where his escape was leading and at the same time to also keep the restaurant's patron happy.

How that could happen remained a decision in the hands of Our Almighty. The distance back home was still too great to get excited so early at this stage. Michael, nevertheless, stopped to plan cautiously ahead. For the moment, he could win food, a bed, roof over his head, and a little daily bonus for his good performance would help Michael, too. To go any further from here meant, however, he would encounter many more people from now on. More people could mean less open but more close doors for him.

At the moment, it remained for Michael more important to secure what he had achieved so far. It was no doubt what he exactly experienced in Chelyabinsk. At that time, the place was still a small town at the foothills of the mighty Ural Mountains, which stretched over a long distance from the south to the far north. The area already supported, for quite some time, the developments of the larger cities of Moscow like Leningrad (Sankt Petersburg) located farther west.

Also at that time, Michael arrived from, mainly, uninhabited Siberia. A plan was considered to develop this remote part of Russia, preferably by prisoners of war. This was once backbreaking work under extreme conditions. The price turned out too high for many prisoners that they couldn't return home alive or not at all. Michael was still working to get himself out of this straight jacket dilemma.

Meanwhile, the life in Chelyabinsk continued its path like ever before in a slow but steady progress. The Second World War didn't make it that far. Ukraine marked the first inhumane signs of the war. Only later, Michael learned that the war hadn't stopped even in Transylvania, leaving its marks behind. It encouraged Michael so much more to stick to a plan, which would enabled him to succeed further with courage. Therefore, he didn't mind working in the restaurant all seven days of the week. That way, he gained his satisfaction and strength, which could carry him better towards his wanted goal.

No rumbling hungry stomach anymore, a good night's sleep in a proper bed, and his appreciated work, they were all the columns Michael was building his nearest future on.

When was the best time to move on from there? Winter still ruled till in this part of the world. In another three months, most of its cold, including the snow, was going to disappear. By then, April would be around. Like all the years before, the spring would arrive with its milder temperatures and its renewed fresh green found mainly in the leaves on trees, which played the waiting game together with the conifers. The heavy white snow caps on the broad branches increasingly released a fresh nice green.

A look through the restaurant's windows displayed a world of mountains where forests had taken a foothold again. An eye-catching scenery after so much endless Siberian space of hardly any change, especially during the long-lasting period of a winter. Michael didn't want to be sidetracked unnecessarily from his set goal. That the scenery belonged to the locals, Michael convinced himself, and it had to be sufficient. He had to stay alert not to exchange his priorities with something else. "Don't tell me, I am a lot of rubbish," Michael reminded himself. Well considered, Michael ensured that even his daily small bonus ended up as his sock savings. A flat wallet around his waist fixed by a belt, kept his hard-earned rubbles secure. This money was intended for Michael to progress his escape. The previous efforts couldn't continue if he wanted to tackle the, by far, still much farther remaining distance home alive and well.

Michael must have remembered that he will face the borders of Ukraine, Moldova, and finally the border of Romania on his escape. Borders mean that own regulations apply there. Before the first border, Michael wanted to use the railway transport from now on as a regular passenger. The luck he had in Siberia didn't mean it would continue in that changing environment. While thinking about all these implications, Michael changed his mind and extended his stay at the restaurant for another three months. This should give him enough time to inform the restaurant's patrons. He hesitated for quite a while to talk about his plan too early. Michael considered some prior warning important when kindness would not suffer a setback to understand each other. Isn't it true that everybody is also the master of his own luck?

Michael's move had not happened at that point yet; his cards still remained off the table. Daily life continued regularly so far, which must have pleased the patron couple too. It was a pleasure for everybody because the number of people who visited the restaurant stayed surprisingly high, and the work load was handled on more than the patron's shoulders only.

Once a month, the evening of music took place. It has come to the point that Michael was the one to inform the patron couple two days in advance about the event. Everything needed its own preparation because nothing could had worked otherwise to satisfaction. The patrons could only say, "Luckily, we have you, Igor. But will the day also arrive when we don't have you anymore?"

Somebody must have had certainly an idea what might happen. Who knows? Michael was not prepared to tell the whole truth and what he had in mind.

It didn't take long for the three months to go past. Michael became increasingly nervous. How could he possibly tell the patron couple his news? Did the other side already smell a rat? Was the news more or less already out?

Michael couldn't hide his behavior, no matter how small the changes looked like. To limit disappointments, Michael decided to speak to the patroness straight away the first thing the next morning with only with a few words, as much as his limited knowledge of the Russian language allowed, "Madam, I got a family too and need to move on from here."

The reply came straightaway, "It's a pity that we are going to lose you. Could you please stay with us for another month? So, we can at least try to find a replacement, which we know will not be easy. When you can agree with my suggestion, I will talk to my husband, and I'm pretty sure he will also agree."

"No problem. I'll keep you in my good memories," Michael responded. He had prepared himself for this moment for quite some time.

The patron remained silent even after a few days, keeping his cool, expressing himself, "In today's world, everything is possible, and we've only to take care that also something good can come out of it, and we can continue."

Another month went almost in a hurry. Michael put even more efforts into his waiter's work to ease the burden for the patron couple before his departure. At his farewell, he didn't even notice if his replacement had shown up.

Besides all that, Michael had also to look at the local railway station when a train was leaving for his desired direction. The time around lunch time seemed to be the best and most suitable one, as Michael's working hours began right afterwards. When he arrived at the local station, he watched carefully not to become unnecessarily noticed. A preliminary enquiry informed him how far his pocket money for the train could bring him. The name of Saratov appeared on a wall map, a good distance away. While talking to the ticket officer, he learned that only the name of his destination was required. Other notifications like Third Class were not asked. His pair of skis came as luggage on the train, free of charge. Michael then booked the train during the week, which helped him to save more. In the end, he was happy that some money was left.

The day of Michael's departure still had to arrive. It happened quicker than even he could have dreamed of. Who became more anxious now? Michael or the patron couple? Both sides appeared calm.

The train was due to run on Wednesday morning. Nobody expected the train to run exactly on time. Passengers were, however, well advised to arrive at the station early enough before the train's arrival.

Michael had, on his way to the station, unexpected company. The patrons insisted to accompany their waiter to the next step in his life. At this stage, it could have been hardly the right time to consider whether this step went into a right direction or not. Michael convinced himself of that.

Arriving together at the station, the patrons couldn't wait for the arrival of the train because they had their restaurant on their mind to not leave it unattended for too long. Then at the station, Michael shook hands with the patron, but the patroness couldn't resist a gentle hug with Michael. The patroness also provided Michael with some food in his newly bought backpack, which was almost hidden. Michael could hardly stop tears from running down his cheeks.

Even the weather joined in the farewell with sunshine. It was now balmy outside for a change. Spring already showed its pleasant side, displaying increasing color. This demonstrated again that in life everything is neither only bad nor good. It depends also on us how we correct circumstances with others. The end result will then be easier for everybody to cope with. In a similar context, it is also said that you are treated as you treat others. It echoes back as you shout into the forest.

REGULAR DEPARTURE WITH THE TRAIN

When the train finally arrived, quite some time had already passed since the patrons had returned to their restaurant. Michael was now about to experience a different kind of travelling. Officially with a ticket in his hand, he could join the other passengers in entering the train. The more affordable third-class carriages appeared with a clear number "3" written on the outside.

The train stopped only for a short time because it was already delayed. One carriage started the next one with a push into the direction until an even speed was achieved.

That had worked for Michael until now. He was well advised to hang on, under those different circumstances. Michael's qualities, such as his modesty, not very noticeable appearance, listening always before saying something, had put him in positions, from when even he as a prisoner of war had found enough room to bring him further into a direction where liberty dawned.

Back to the railway journey: As could only be expected, people who expressed their enjoyment with a lot of noise had also entered the train. They were probably people who hadn't travelled much on a train. The train's timber floor had to accept many dancing feet. Some of the passengers knew how to add their voices to the dancing feet. It, of course, couldn't last forever because the ticket control, on its regular train inspection, felt obliged to stop such nonsense. Time didn't fail to bring back peace and quiet. In the end, this kind of fun could become only the exemption because other passengers like Michael tried to think about something else, for instance thoughts about his homecoming and how it could be fulfilled.

Michael kept quiet. He had no problem with other people's different opinions. For him, it became important not to get involved with a discussion which might become obvious that he was a stranger. Nobody showed any interest in Michael; that's why he had reason enough to remain on his own.

While the train rolled through the countryside, springtime added already new colourful life into the monotonous white scenery of the winter. Michael had enough time to arrange his thoughts. This time, there was no challenge to the limit of what he could bear. How his escape would continue when getting closer to the borders of the neighboring countries—Ukraine and Moldova. A question mark remained most likely between the Russian and Romanian borders.

Michael's thoughts kept him busy, *If I try to have an idea of Russia's territorial size and vastness, considering what I've experienced so far, I ask myself: Why can't people live in peace?*

More respect for life in general could help save unnecessary loss of lives. Always the innocent ones had to pay with their lives for the miscalculations of the others. The ones who claim responsibility are mainly the ones causing the troubles. They also know how to retreat into secure positions. Aren't the politician with the rich people the ones to secure their positions?

I have to admit as long as I was busy enough, such thoughts didn't cross my mind. Only the distance to so much nonsense makes us think first better about our lives, when we can look back to some more secure background. Neither the train nor the passengers could luckily read other people's thoughts. It is also here a proof that the thoughts can remain free, no matter what conditions somebody is in.

The "circus" of the passengers at the beginning of the departure settled itself as quickly as it had started. No train control had to keep an eye on order and discipline anymore. For Michael, it became a resting time when he could connect his thoughts from the past to the near future.

How could his way of thinking be classified as a peasant? He could easily prove that he was on the right track until recently, which could be considered an intelligent one. He had a simple understanding that all that intellect could go to the moon, where it would cause less harm. Michael reassured himself easily that his work followed a more natural path.

As Michael was now a regular passenger on a train, it was the result of many earlier efforts. The end could also teach him how everything really happened. He was now happy enough when he looked out of the train's window and saw how the springtime returned the nature into a new more colourful dress. *Something good should come out for me as well,* thought Michael wishfully.

SARATOV - BELGOROD BY TRAIN

Time already took care of it and was passing quickly enough, so that Michael could arrive in Saratov as a regular passenger on a train. It remained important, however, to not lose any valuable time. Saratov station also had a ticket office. On the wall of the station, hung a map indicating where all trainlines were leading to.

The two days on the train proved that Michael was going to win a considerable distance closer to home. The food from the patroness sufficiently provided what Michael's stomach needed.

The map on the wall showed farther south, at the Ukrainian border, a place called Belgorod. It felt like travelling a few days on the train. Now arose the question: Will Michael's last pocket money carry him still so far? The answer could only be delivered by the person behind the ticket office window. Full of expectations, Michael awaited the answer after he had told his destination as clearly as he could through the window. The price appeared now on the ticket. Michael knew straightaway whether or not he had enough money. Believe it or not, the money was just enough. It was all that counted for the moment.

Michael arrived in Saratov around midday. His next departure time was only a few hours later in the afternoon. While walking repeatedly up and down the platform in front of the station, he easily forgot about the past long hours sitting on the train. Neither the other people waiting around the station nor himself disturbed each other. Most of these waiting passengers were preoccupied with a travel plan, certainly of a different nature, like he was. During his waiting time, Michael picked up other words than Russian. No matter how great Michael's escape appeared to him, the Soviet Union of that time reached much farther almost into all directions.

Indeed, a new steam engine with a number of carriages arrived as planned at Saratov station. Not only passenger compartments but also goods carriages made up the train. Some carriages were visibly loaded to the top with black coal near the steam engine, a reminder from where Michael had arrived. An extra load of coal must have accompanied the train, making sure that enough power was available for the whole distance.

Michael was not alone in a train's compartment when the station master signalled the departure with his round red shield on a wooden rod. It didn't take place exactly in line with the timetable, but it happened anyway. The station master's special cap helped underline the event's importance. Michael didn't fail to reassure himself that the train was running to his wanted direction.

The carriage of class three was packed this time with passengers. Michael had to watch and secure one place for himself. Above the passengers were luggage carriers, which were more than enough to keep Michael's skis safe and sound.

There was now a lot of time available to just look out of the window and experience how the world looked like there during daylight. Snow and its cold had already disappeared quite a while. Green meadows were disrupted with patches of forest, raised between hillsides and mountain formations. The train had found its way through all of it with full steam.

Stopovers offered occasionally some welcome changes. In the middle of the night, the train stopped at a small station next to another train. From there, the train changed its direction towards the northeast, where it was also far away the large city, Moscow, was located. It was very clear for Michael to not take that direction. There were enough passengers, who changed into the waiting next train. Moscow would have been the wrong direction because Michael would have expected more problems in such a large place, where people live like ants. The direction back was neither on. His goal remained his home in Transylvania.

From now on, Michael watched how, in every next station, more and more passengers left the train. What it meant was up to Michael to find out because he couldn't communicate enough in the Russian language. He wanted neither to compromise his status as an escaped prisoner of war.

The more distance Michael gained from the prisoners' camp, the more he realized that he had come closer to the battlefields of the Second World War, which haunted him more than a year ago when he ended up in Siberia. In the vicinity of Ukraine, the war had already left inhumane marks behind. During his absence, Michael couldn't have known what happened at home. He concluded that from now on, his escape could face more problems. At every station, Michael was keen to find out how much longer he could remain on the train.

Belgorod was finally the station where Michael was well advised to leave the train together with the few remaining passengers. Not long before the passengers left the train, they still behaved freely, and nobody cared about anybody else. Despite this rather large town, a strange silence ruled the area. Michael kept silent, not even trying to ask questions. He left the station together with the other passengers, reassuring himself that this was the best way not to wake somebody's attention. What next? Good advice was in short supply here! Michael couldn't use his skis; there was no snow anymore. He slowly started on foot towards the town center. As he passed a shop window, a great variety of articles were on display, reminding Michael what the use of his skis had become. Could somebody else make use of them in that place? When Michael entered the shop, nobody showed up. Little later, his patience paid off. A lady appeared from the back of a room, approaching Michael near the entrance door. "Good day," Michael wished her anyway. He then showed the lady his skis, and from there they had to speak for themselves. The lady showed no sign of a refusal. On the contrary, with both her hands, she took the skis and the two poles and leaned them against a wall.

In addition to her words, she indicated counting bank notes with the fingers of one of her hands. Michael understood her sign language quite well and responded, "One hundred rubles."

21

BELGOROD, A NEW CITY ENCOUNTER

"This is your idea. I can't give you more than fifty rubles," she said as she took out one fifty ruble out of her cash desk. This situation reminded Michael of the following adages: *A bird in the hand is worth two in the bush; Beggars can't be choosers,* and *Better a sparrow in the hand than a pigeon on the roof.*

He considered the fifty rubles something of value. He quickly worked mentally how many days of basic food he could buy with it. No more words had to be exchanged, and Michael could leave the shop.

He now got rid of his skis, and the shop owner certainly knew a customer who could use them, even in an area where skis were rarely used. Hopefully, luck could have changed hands also this way.

The next nightfall was not far away. Michael now faced the problem of where to spend the night and asked himself, *Shouldn't I have asked the shop owner for a bed to stay overnight?* Only now did it cross his mind that "the proof of the pudding is in the eating." Michael returned to the shop, knocking at the door which was locked this time.

"We are closed now. Tomorrow is another day," the voice from inside the house called out.

I can't have always luck on my side, Michael reassured himself. *I can't, however, leave it like that. A night on the street here is out of the question. In bigger places, especially in a close neighbourhood of the Ukrainian border, you never know what kind of people could be around. Should I try once more and knock at the shop's door? Even if somebody gets upset, it's worth a try.*

That time no voice could be heard from inside the house. The door flew open, and a man stood in front of Michael. Any communication didn't really want to get started at this late hour of the night. The woman Michael first met also appeared on the scene, immediately recognizing Michael again. The presence of a dog that had come closer to the door helped reached a better understanding. The dog was, this time, a real big one, the breed Michael couldn't figure out. Was he probably a crossbreed of a dog and a wolf? The dog remained surprisingly quiet. Could the dog have eventually known more about Michael than words express? The woman gestured to Michael by putting both her hands on one side of her face, asking if Michael was looking for an overnight stay. Michael could only nod his head.

"Well, to stay the night outside is no good for anybody. If the dog has no objections, not much could possibly go wrong. In times of the war, one has to be careful to trust somebody. We have to expect the enemy everywhere. You better come in our house right now.

We don't want to raise unnecessary suspicion. The enemy has inflicted already too much harm. Tomorrow morning, you should better keep moving because both sides, the Russian and the enemy, keep their watchful eyes everywhere."

Warmth in the house was no question anymore. Michael realized that there was work left to clean up for the day in the kitchen. Almost as if he was used to it, Michael went straight to the kitchen's sink, opened the tap after the plug in the sink was put in place, allowing to raise enough water. With hand signs, he gestured where could he find the washing detergent, and all was then ready to go. The tenants were pleased with what they saw, "You must feel like at home when you know so well about housework." This was what the lady had to say, still adding, "Whoever knows how to help must be a good person for sure. And when two sides know to help each other, everybody is happy. After this work in the kitchen, you deserve some refreshment even late in the evening. A hungry stomach doesn't want to go to sleep easily as we all know."

The woman made herself understood while she gestured, taking her hand to her mouth and rubbing the other one over her stomach.

"You should have a good night's sleep now," added the head of the household. "We know already very well that much human suffering remains in the dark. A good night's sleep has always been the best medicine for all of us. I go already to bed and hope the night will pass without disturbances. Our dog is the best guard for it. Let's wish us all a good night, so that a new day can begin well enough. I'm gone already."

Michael knew well enough what to say or not, so the others could understand him. He was probably the first one to fall asleep in a bed of his own.

The next day started with the new daylight. Even if it took a while, Michael got up in a hurry because he realized that the couple was already moving around the house. In a brief encounter, the lady showed Michael where he could find a washing facility, and gesturing by moving her hand to her mouth, which meant they could all have breakfast together. Michael was quite happy with the kind of breakfast he received. A hot cup of tea was more than he could have wished for. It was now time for Michael to take off again. The Russian military with its Secret Service had established a foothold everywhere. Nobody wanted to become a target.

Despite the difficult situation, the shop owners didn't hesitate to give Michael, on top of the tea, something to eat for his way. A friendly handshake indicated farewell for Michael and the couple.

Michael didn't miss to have a closer look at the map while he was still in the shop. At that time, Ukraine had only one official border with Russia. Situated on the other side of Ukraine was the town of Kharkov, which was the shortest distance to his way home. But under no circumstances was Michael prepared to lose his goal because of border controls. A bad day at the border could already jeopardize it. The war supplied the main problems in the first place. Could the situation repeat itself, when Michael found himself trapped at home, leading to his prisoner-of-war situation?

No! Under no circumstances could it repeat itself! Michael's answer to that was to look for a more insignificant border crossing. It could have been his first time back on foot. The night would be the best time to move because of less visibility. Hence, Michael looked for a hay barn in a field where he could stay for the rest of the day. He escaped from Belgorod unseen as fast as he could. Michael had only to wait and see what really was going on. At least so early in the morning, anyone was hardly up and on the move. Away from the road, he had chosen a direction straight into surrounding meadows with low growing bush and in between scattered trees. The trees announced already that springtime was on its way. A question resulted from this: Will the new shoots of life also bring luck for Michael?

Before coming closer to a hay barn, Michael still observed out of a distance that nobody else was around. He saw nobody, so he entered the cooler shadow interior of the barn through a half-opened door. The air there was filled with a strong scent of hay. An invitation to lie down and wait how the day will go presented itself. The weather too showed its bright face; only a few clouds hovered in the sky.

As soon as daylight was on the verge of going away, Michael took his direction on foot towards the south, the direction he established around midday when the sun stood high up in the sky. To exercise caution every moment then on was dictated to Michael. He was even keen and considered his first attempt to cross the border to Ukraine. If everything was running well, a decision to continue will come closer on hand. *In case an uncertainty would arise, pull back in time and try again,* thought Michael to himself.

Not much light the night sky received at this time of the year. The night was, therefore, almost pitch dark. Carefully and silently, Michael was seeking, step by step, a way through meadows, fields, and bushes. Michael paid special attention to a possible encounter with a border control accompanied by a watchdog. Michael had to become aware of the dog first to eventually escape in time, as long as he was on Russian territory.

FIRST BORDER CROSSING INTO UKRAINE

Michael must have somehow reached territory of the Ukraine. The night remained silent and dark; no interruption had taken place. Michael felt relief; however, he remained cautious with a too early joy. He must have reached already land away from the border when he found himself on a bitumen road leading into the south. The first bigger city in Ukraine territory was Kharkov, which he avoided, leaving it in the east alone.

How to continue on his escape became an important question for Michael. From then on, he found himself in enemy territory where war had left its marks. Michael had not much of a saying when eventually confronted by weapon's opposition. More importantly, it became for him a reminder to stay out of such confrontation.

It was rather safer on foot than it was an easy journey; otherwise, it was the only option that Michael could keep for the moment, until something else would turn up. What Michael had gained to get out of "hell", he could not jeopardized under any circumstance.

The next morning, daylight revealed where Michael found himself. A border crossing was nearby; a watchful eye was needed to not overlook potential minefields that disrupt control border crossings. In this respect, Michael had worked out the following ideas: A mine on his way would certainly had put an end to his escape. The location of mines he could not be able to find out. A close look around was the only option for Michael. He assumed that flat country invites a better border crossing; whereas, hills are more in the way for this purpose. In the end, it is left to every individual intending to cross a border, to decide whether or not they want to run this kind of risk.

Regarding Michael's situation, he was bound to be fox and rabbit at the same time. Michael paid maximum attention to noises and changes with his eyes and ears, especially during the darkness of the night.

The Ukraine belonged to the Soviet Union in 1942. They were much the same people. The Russian language, more or less, unified the countries at that time. It was the foreign military that introduced the "bone of contents." Much later in the beginning of 2000, the conflict broke out with Russia. Nobody was prepared to give way anymore; the result became, so far, a devastation of Ukraine and terrible losses of life on both sides. At the time when Michael had entered Ukraine, the conflict hadn't developed to such a degree, luckily.

Michael still managed to enter Ukraine unseen. A bitumen road leading into the southwest direction became the best welcome sign of the early day break for Michael. He was well advised to change his way of an escape from then on. Solely on foot would have taken too long. What other possibilities were available? Everything related to military was out of question. Michael didn't want to appear like a beggar on the road side. This could have become more of an invitation for a control. Therefore, he decided to walk away from the road on a distance that he could still see a car on the road. Somebody far and wide alone on foot is more likely to invite a helpful driver to stop.

And indeed, still on daylight, a car stopped on the level with Michael. In Russian, Michael was instructed, "Get in quickly if you want to come with me. We don't want to becom a military target here.

Somebody who pushes his way on foot along the road to get farther is worth a helping hand. This is how I think, what do you think?"

Said and it was straight done! Michael couldn't believe his luck.

While Michael was sitting in a car which moved him much more comfortably and quicker, the Ukraine driver thought about how they could communicate with each other. He tried in few Romanian words, explaining, "We've been for quite some time good neighbors. In Romania, people commonly speak more than one language. My wife by the way speaks also German. She originates from Germany, speaking Siebenbürgen."

Michael jumped up out of joy at the news, he responded in German too, "This is pure luck."

The driver continued, "Here in the Ukraine, a war is going on. Fortunately, I live far enough outside the capital of Kiev. So far, we haven't become a target. It's always the same. People like you and I never have a reason to fight each other. It's always the politicians starting a fight for no obvious reason. They always cause trouble, which ends up only with huge losses. Tonight, you better stay with us. I wonder what my wife has to say to our visitor.

Tomorrow morning I'll contact a nearby friend who occasionally drives to Moldova. I know he will help you to get you farther. This only proves that help always gets us farther than war. We must, however, remain watchful not to end up in a wrong place at a wrong time because war is not forgiving."

The day would deliver a good driving distance. A break at a right time was also not forgotten. The car received petrol from time to time that was welcomed by its passengers, so they could relax their feet, at least by doing a little walking. Passengers and the car arrived at the destination before it was beginning to get dark. No control occurred which could have caused some major headache. The war kept its firing power back for other occasions.

Who has become anxious now? Most likely, nobody more than Michael. The unforeseen encounter with somebody from home couldn't be more exciting. And this already so much closer to Michael's home! However, it hasn't been close enough yet; more patience was still required.

The driver's house stood alone in the region, surrounded by large wheat fields freshly ploughed and harrowed with seeds as far as the eye could see. At that time, fields were not interesting enough to become part of a war. Michael had inherited this knowledge. Usually, a peasant tends to live life in a more modest way, contented with what he has and is, therefore, less contested. Peasant work is not much recognized anyway.

The welcome at the driver's house was as friendly as it only could be, although nobody has been seen before nor has come across each other. Also here, coincidences supported a positive outcome in a more open environment than in a densely populated area.

FIRST ENCOUNTER WITH HOME COUNTRY

The moment the driver, whose name had to be kept concealed out of consideration for Michael, introduced his wife to Michael, in a broken Saxon dialect. This was only proof enough for her that Michael also called Transylvania (Siebenbürgen) his home.

After this heartfelt welcome, Michael didn't tell how he came there. Too much worried him that something could still go wrong. At least for the time being, it didn't look like it. The housewife came out with the invitation, "We have dinner together tonight, don't we? Has our guest a special wish? How about something that reminds us of Siebenbürgen (Transylvania)?"

"Everything, what such helpful hands can do, is more than welcome," replied Michael.

"How about a pea soup with sausages as starters and afterwards pancakes with jam. This should be enough for a stomach to love," responded the housewife.

After the stomach was satisfied, the next step was to have a good night's sleep. Michael was very surprised after going to a not him familiar bed that he closed his eyes straightaway to a wonderful deep sleep. Whether his dreams were good, bad, or existing at all, he couldn't remember the next morning.

Michael was so much more impressed with such kindness from people whom he just met accidentally, not even at home, but one could almost say "in a wild field." To be honest, during the war, we are all more or less "in a wild field." Nevertheless, it was and still is worthwhile to find back to reconciliation because it essentially supports life to continue even against all odds.

"A new day, a new person" was how Michael felt after a long good night's sleep.

As Michael didn't want to let people know his real name, the same was with his host. In the late history to date, Ukraine experienced a suffering from hunger, which was used as a weapon under Stalin, until the mass executions under the command of Hitler. History never taught us anything; everything repeated itself, with the only exemption of an increased suffering.

The war again made people insecure to that extent that "hiding places" for openness and trust were difficult to find. At least one hand had found something reliable, it was much easier for the other hand to stretch out farther. In that sense, Michael wanted to carry on with his escape.

A friend of the previous driver used to drive regularly into Moldova, in the "shadow" of the war events, a small country in the west of Ukraine. This friend turned up very early the next morning in front of the frontdoor of Michael's host. How a communication could have taken place in those days, honestly, remained a mystery. Michael also had on his mind to cross the border to Romania via Moldova. At that time, Russia wasn't too much present in those border areas.

The weather showed still its sunny side, the air was warm enough, although rain clouds appeared on the far horizon. The farewell from the driver host's home was short and fast because nobody needed to know what was going on there. Even a helping hand could have been misunderstood and could be misinterpreted as an enemy action. The apparent peace at that moment could also have been the calm before the storm.

The new driver used a middle-sized truck on which he delivered goods in an exchange for something else. Michael didn't show any interest on what it was. This driver also spoke the Romanian language like Michael. Something worth interesting to notice is how people could still communicate across borders despite the waged war.

A communication with this driver didn't start easily, although both sides were able to communicate in the Romanian language. The area compensated for it with its views of a natural still unchanged environment. When it was before the wide, open wheat fields of Ukraine, the scenery changed gradually into the foothills of the Carpathian Mountain ring. Ukraine has excellent soil, thanks to geological influences when from far away distances, the ice age had shifted volcanic activities to this wide, open land delta all the way through Siberia into Ukraine. A similar situation can be found with the La Pampa in Argentina, where the rich soil brings a great harvest on huge land areas.

After the Carpathians, Transylvania is located inside its mountain ring, where ancient floods had created a rich soil countryside with wide spread forests. Romania experienced similar geological changes with its Danube River course and delta, where the large fields of the Baragan Plain deliver rich harvests.

Let's get not too far ahead but rather remain connected with Michael's present reality. Somehow and sometime later, the truck finally arrived at the border of Moldova. Michael became quite unsettled before the border because he considered it to be an increased security risk for himself. As the driver spoke the Romanian language, a mutual understanding would at least result out of it. The driver spoke out frankly out, "Don't worry. The people at the border know me already for many years, reaching an agreement every time with some mutual support. In our case you will be my driver."

Much was also at that time possible in this world, only the right cooperation had to join.

In the most northern part of Moldova only an insignificant border crossing waited for Michael and the driver. Nevertheless, one secret kept this border mainly begging for attention like the other ones do. The driver knew about it from experience. It was the day when no control took place. Like well-known friends, the few border posts exchanged only greetings.

Borders were, at that time, simply the result of wheelings and dealings. Its population was much less involved, marginally differing on both sides. In Moldova, the Romanian border came closer quickly. The driver entrusted Michael to manage the last distance on foot. The driver didn't want to see his mission disrupted somehow.

The horizon showed up already in the snow-covered high mountain tops of the Carpathians in the west. The parting between the truck driver and Michael took place quickly so as not to draw unnecessary attention. Michael was from now on set free on his own feet again. During the lift with the truck, Michael satisfied his hungry stomach. Michael made it so far till there. To get any farther became no question whatsoever for Michael. What changed hands from the truck was of no interest for Michael. He moved towards the side of the road as quickly as possible so as not to be noticed. No bitumen road that time. Still a good rest from tiredness and an empty stomach accompanied Michael from then on.

Near a single house, Michael slowed down his pace. He stopped opposite the house, looked around in all directions, thinking to himself, *If somebody lived in the house, he must have appeared rather helpless to him.*

A man walked out of the house, shouting at Michael, "What is a Romanian gypsy doing here? Go to hell!"

That was enough for Michael. He knew very clearly that this was not a place to ask for a stay.

At springtime, the grass was lush green and visibly high out. Then, half an hour later on foot, Michael met a farmer in a field who collected grass equally spaced in heaps. The "grass spoke" to Michael, and without hesitating, he approached the farmer, "Do you need a helping hand? It doesn't hurt to receive help from time to time."

"This sounds almost too good to be true. I can't remember when was the last time that somebody offered me a helping hand." The farmer let Michael understand while he continued collecting grass with the pitchfork.

"When you really mean what you are telling me, take my pitchfork, and watch how I turn and collect the grass. Don't tell me that you already know how to handle the hay. Are you also a farmer from the other side of the border?"

"When it comes to a helping hand, I handle this as easy as a pie."

"Here we are. Show me what you can do. There is enough hay to put your hands on." The other farmer took, from his wagon with two horses, another pitch fork, and the work started in no time.

The two horses had, in front of them, mixed grain and hay in a bag above the ground to keep them busy and calm. The horses didn't take notice of Michael at all. It looked like he belonged to their team. The farmer noticed it though, adding, "He who knows how to help must be a good person. How it happened that you arrived here is not so important. During the war, too many people get mixed up. That's why answers to questions are not needed. They create only more confusion. At home, bread, bacon and the new wine from last autumn is already waiting for us. My wife, including our two children, is also there. When they will see you and learn how good you've helped me, there will also certainly be some food left for you. If you like, you could also stay the night with us. The next day, the hay work will not go away. If you can also help me tomorrow, we'll get to the Romanian border together with a full load of hay and the two horses. Only then you'll take the reins into your hands, while I, the "boss" will sit next to you and answer any questions that might arise. In the countryside with its fields, nobody will keep a too close eye on what is happening here. Even the Russian military from farther away haven't shown up yet. Before the darkness catches up with us again, we better get back to my house, which is still located on the Moldovan territory."

The closer Michael came to the Romanian border, the more expectations had built up hope that *Ochotska Sibir* would come to an end very soon. He had not yet come close enough to it. His stay in a house for a change with a family encouraged Michael to keep going. A big question mark was hanging over his situation at home. What did his family look like? The only answer could be: One more cautious step at the time.

Besides all this, Michael couldn't miss, during his stay with the family, the traditionally colourful embroidery of curtains and cushions around a sofa, table cloths, artistic wall shelves that were proof of a diligence in creating something and having an effect on a more contentious, happier life in the country. At that time, people there were proud to pass on something of their own to the next generation, like at home in Transylvania. Consume brought changes especially in this respect, which was born in a progress understanding. A little more of a simple life and diligence has always helped to keep people united together.

Back in the family's home, sweet corn with fried chicken was served on the table. This helped the evening pass in a flash. Michael found peace in a bed of his own for this night, too.

Here in the countryside people were used to a more quiet life than in more densely populated areas. Whether the rooster here also crowed also to announce an early morning, Michael couldn't remember anymore. What was sure, however, was that work on the field and the meadows was already waiting without a doubt. That's why life had returned into the house in an instance.

"When we collect hay early enough, we should be able to still bring it home before the rain will comes. Our snack will then become our breakfast at the same time."

Michael had thoughts of his own, too. He took the opportunity and spoke out, "The idea that I should take over the horses' reins is, in my opinion, not a good one because the horses don't know me well enough. How will they react at the border in case something might not go according to plan? You are so kind to me. Let's keep it simple. I'm suggesting that we drive together with our wagon full of hay close to the border as usual, and you better keep the reins. Do you know somebody on the other side of the border who needs your hay? In mountainous areas, good hay is much more in short supply. Our hay wagon will also divert attention easily. I'm going to use the time to cross the Moldavian border farther away undetected. The next border to Romania, I will tackle somehow anyway. No matter what we decide, it remains important that none of us gets into unforeseen trouble. You help me, and it's understood that I show consideration also for you. What is your opinion?"

"Peasant's craftiness must be well known to you. Who knows what you have already achieved with it so far. We probably should cross the Romanian border together because the farther my hay can travel, the more valuable it can become. Let's stop talking and get our load of hay ready, so we can reach our goal earlier. I got more than enough hay, which we know already is short in supply in the Carpathian Mountains."

The hay wagon owner knew the area quite well. Therefore, he was also known to many other people. Ultimately, it was still important who occupied the border control at this time. The peace and quiet there already helped much in dealing with more secrecy. Minefields were not set up in such remote areas.

24

BORDER CROSSING MOLDAVIA - ROMANIA

Michael was again quickly on foot a good distance away from the border control. The hay wagon with the horses must have passed the border already. Not long after the border, the two peasants met again.

"Jump on to my wagon's front. Together, we can still go farther."

The rain had, so far, hesitated to fall. The border control preferred to stay dry, which was better for their guns as well as for them.

With Transylvanian home ground under his feet, mountain peaks of the Carpathians reaching high into the sky and bottoms of valleys seeking ways through dense forests, Michael had to be mindful of meeting bears looking for berries. Best in such a situation was not to panic but rather to pretend as if somebody else was out for berries and leave the bears alone.

Michael had something else on his mind, which were neither the bears nor the berries. He was after a bitumen road where he possibly could meet a car that could give him a lift. He thought to himself, *Better a less comfortable ride in a car than a long walk on foot. Let's see!*

Michael had lost the contact with the hay wagon by now, thinking even further that the other peasant had, meanwhile, found a buyer for his hay load.

The year had already reached the month of June. The darkness of a night couldn't be kept away. The Carpathians peaks dominated far and wide and shone on the sky. The question now arose for Michael: Where could he stay overnight in that darkness? Next question would be: How would he proceed to the direction of his home the following day? The highest mountain peaks reached already two thousand meters and in some places even surpassing it. The highest parts were covered in white snow, which didn't melt away even during the summer. Michael knew that he had to prepare himself for a chilly night. There was no hope anymore with the increasing darkness. At the foot of an grown old oak tree, Michael prepared a spot with the few surrounding fir tree branches to lie down during the night. His stomach had to be contended for the time being with an outlook for another day.

Only in the night's darkness Michael learned that, surprisingly, he was not alone. An owl and a cuckoo announced to the other forest inhabitants that a foreigner had come to us. Michael had no interest in meeting a wolf or a bear. More importantly, it remained that the silence in the forest was not disrupted by somebody who was unwanted. The next morning appeared on the horizon early. Firstly, little light shone through then increasingly to full sunshine but not so much in the forest.

Don't let the stomach have its say now. I managed so far till here. I'm almost home. God help me a little longer, these thoughts passed Michael's mind. Had the cold of Siberia secretly accompanied Michael?

Whether Michael liked it or not, the voice of his stomach didn't go away. The bear searching for berries reminded him of a possible food source. Only a few footsteps away from his resting place, he found blue berries in the green grass and the partly low bush. Looking closer, the increasing daylight revealed a full carpet of blue berries. *Isn't this something already? Now the bears should only leave me alone, so my stomach will enjoy them, too.* Michael said to himself.

To think any further so early in the morning was not on Michael's mind. He also said to himself, reminding him of his homecoming, *Rather the sparrow in my hand then the pigeon on the roof.* He had given priority to find a road, a passage which allowed him to get further; however, the rain was not helpful at all. This was actually the first time that Michael experienced rain during his escape from the prisoners' camp. Now, his new backpack experienced an unusual application. It didn't hold anything much useful to eat any more, but when held flat over the head, it helped keep much of the rain away.

After some time had passed, when the road was partially leading up and down, a strange vehicle arrived from behind, came to a halt in the middle of the road just on the side of Michael.

The Romanian words couldn't be properly understood on either side as the rain interrupted much of a conversation. What, however, came through were these words, "You poor bugger. Leave the rain behind, and join me in my cabin. Where do you want to go?"

Words of such an invitation couldn't go unheard. Behind the driver's seat was timber stored directly on the side of an oven. Its chimney was going on a short distance up into the air. This indicated that for a continued trip, enough heating material had come on board. During the Second World War as well as during the first one, public vehicles were not commonly seen on roads unlike in later years of development. During the time of Michael's escape from Siberia, vehicles were mainly running for the military. Unfortunately, the military became the development driving force there. Whether it was leading to something better, the future will only be able to tell.

Exactly as the wooden carburettor came with its *tock, tock, tock* to a halt, the chimney-motor started again with a *tock, tock, tock.*

Independent from Michael's luck might also be of interest for our descendants how restrictions, especially through wartimes, supported developments of cars with the wood carburettor motor. The author writes about it because he experienced himself during and after World

War II, the development of the wooden carburettor motor even when he was a child.

During this *tock, tock, tock* trip, wood had to be added to the burning motor in regular intervals and distances. It was also needed to stop from time to time and collect more branches from the nearby forest, which fitted into the vehicle's loading platform. This happened fairly quickly with their joined forces because Michael knew well enough to work with an axe and a saw.

On the road going long uphill, the oven of the motor had difficulties to keep the vehicle running. The answer was to feed more timber and wait a while each time. Sometimes, the motor started again, continuing the trip. The experience from this became: Take your time, and do not waste it.

The answer for Michael on how to get closer to his home could not rely only on simply feeding timber into a carburettor motor anymore. Signs of the escape difficulties from Siberia showed increasingly on Michael. Not even a day would Michael consider it as a normal one. The escape itself was already a highly dangerous undertaking. The necessities of a daily life like keeping yourself clean, clothes in order, no word about brushing teeth, or even sipping in the morning from a barrel of his own schnapps were missing. All these were challenges of which the weight became only apparent with time. More likely, it also became the trigger for many encounters with others on why the consideration and sympathy could take place. It showed, how such basic elements could succeed; there was no need of a war.

A key question had arisen for Michael: How well had he escaped from the war and its consequences? A possible answer lies on a difference of individual people's perceptions. One or the other answer might be at the end of a tunnel, where we all move together in an attempt to reach a goal. Some individuals try the exemption to find his/her own way in a life. It is how a summary of life could be regarded.

Michael had chosen a happy medium to share life on his road, not only with human species but also with animals. Now his efforts have come closer to an end result The ultimate touchstone had arrived: Was his escape a success? One consolation was that he stood again on home ground. The northern part of Romania, namely Transylvania, looked much smaller but nevertheless rich and beautiful in comparison to some parts of Russia like Siberia.

To catch a transport at home in Transylvania was something Michael didn't really expect at all. The Saxon dialect helped Michael communicate there with other people. The one who spoke the Saxon dialect was considered, from the beginning, one of them. The first important destination for Michael was Mediasch, where the circle of events led him to Siberia, came to a close. From now on, he moved for the next few days on foot, on a cart pulled by horses or cows. Michael had to also admit that never before had he come that far outside of his hometown of Kleinschelken. These kinds of observations had to remain limited because Michael had to concentrate and pull his last strength together if he wanted his escape to come to an end. If wanted or not, he was left more on his own when it came to what he could expect at home.

Michael arrived in Mediasch on foot during the day. In the market place, he looked around for acquaintances he could eventually remember. He could hardly believe that it could become a difficult task for him now. What had happened here? Did he change so much, or had the war changed the people? Michael didn't want to stay in such a central place for much longer. No military personnel could, however, be seen in a first instant, but Michael didn't want to run the risk and jeopardize his arrival.

Outside of Mediasch seemed to be a more promising possibility of meeting somebody Michael could still recognize from Kleinschelken. A view from too close often becomes restricted. Very soon Michael found himself amongst other people on foot on the road, leading out of Mediasch. As fellow sufferers together on the road, words were easier exchanged. This time again it was a horse and cart that invited Michael to hop on. Unlike before, Michael missed the cart's front because he simply lacked strength.

"You must have already come a long distance. Wait, I stop, so that you can better join me. Who is this I see? Is this Michael from Kleinschelken? I must stop completely and find out who has so badly beaten Michael up."

"This is such a long story, and I'm only happy that at last it's over. Nobody wants to experience something as bad, let alone to hear about it," responded Michael.

"All that I know is that nobody has seen you around for quite some time. I can't believe that you were also deported to Siberia. Let's better forget it. What you need, everybody can see it. The best is, I drop you off at the church fortress, and you will meet the pastor, who will know for sure what you need. I can't tell more, it's only bad news."

ARRIVAL IN KLEINSCHELKEN

The fortress walls and the two great towers the war could not take away easily. The road leading along the Kockel riverbed pointed to the direction where Michael's farmhouse was located. Later, Michael learned why there was no word his family at home was awaiting him. He followed the advice of the previous horse cart driver to see the pastor first. Who this driver was, Michael couldn't remember anymore. He must have been a good person from when, during war times, only a few were still around.

Why see the pastor? In Transylvanian villages, the pastor played an important role. He was the one who knew about everything and everybody—from birth till death. He was also educated and an example of a good believer in Luther, the reformer of the church. Family matters, school, hunger, hardships, illnesses, weddings, baptisms, church services, community celebrations—on all these occasions the pastor played his leading role.

Such a firm belief in God also resulted in a unique defense without waging war, such could be found in the areas of Tibet and certain parts of the Indigenous Americans. In Transylvania, the Saxons had already built fortresses from the twelfth century where they retreated and defended themselves against all kind of raids from far and wide. Inside the church ring fortress, every peasant had allocated his own place with some harvest stored away. This back up enabled the defenders within the church fortress to outlast an aggressor most of the time until the former could starve the latter out.

The interior of these churches reflected on the devotion in a belief of a village. To date, the center of the church shows, in most cases, wooden benches going across side archways, the font, the altar that are all equally distanced, opposite to it at the other end stands out a beautiful organ from which some of the oldest originals of the world belong. An ornate big bell in the tower called the village inhabitants to devotions and prayers and still does.

The pastor was at home. Michael didn't need to explain himself. The pastor already knew too much about what the village of Kleinschelken had to suffer. The time was not right to pass the bad news on. Hope needed fresh nourishment. Considering the present situation, the pastor first grabbed the practical sides of life. He asked Michael to stay the night with him. Michael's appearance already said enough of how he could hang on to life with his strong belief in God. When all human power reaches an end, only faith in something higher will survive.

The pastor lived together with a few other important villagers in the direct neighborhood of the church fortress. At that very moment, the church could not have been the right place for Michael. In the pastor's home was enough room to comfort one of the community's most worn out faithfuls, enabling him to continue with his life. It was good for Michael to find a more normal life with some necessary distance, because what else was awaiting him, he couldn't know yet.

Later the next morning, Michael became fully aware that he was at home again in Kleinschelken. His memory could tell him only little about the day when he was forced to leave for Siberia and what a *cock-a-doodle-do* announced that morning. Today, however, nothing happened. What could that mean? Had the pastor's home been too far out of the way for a rooster?

As soon as Michael was restored to some degree with the help of the pastor and his wife, together they prepared Michael for what awaited him at their table. Unfortunately, it was not good news. The pastor decided to pass first to Michael the most important message on that his wife, Sara, did not survive the birth of their second son, Martin.

"Do you want me to accompany you to the grave of your wife? You need also to know that your son Martin is alive with the God's help. Remember, not everything is only bad in a life. Where hope can meet belief, much still remains, as you've experienced during your courageous escape from Siberia. The best is that we go to the cemetery as early as possible, before the life in our village starts."

In the village of Kleinschelken, the path to the cemetery was, at that time, still a short distance away from the village's center. At the very end of the cemetery, the pastor stopped in front of a grave that had not yet received a complete layout. "It's here where we've laid her to rest in the God's hands. The war hasn't allowed to pay more attention to this grave. Learn to get along with life from here, not only for yourself but for both of your sons, too. I know this fate is difficult to bear for anyone. I better leave you alone from now on, so you can find peace and quiet again. God bless you and His kindness shall stay with you, amen."

Michael had reached a point where he didn't know anymore where he had arrived. First Siberia then this kind of a homecoming, why did it have to be like that? Down on his knees, many tears fell on to the grave of his wife, Sara. It helped, however, to become a relief for Michael to reach a new determination and not give up but to continue his life. Next came the path to his home. Already at a distance, Michael didn't miss that the front gates towards the yard were left wide open. *What does that mean? Should I be prepared for more bad news?* crossed Michael's mind.

Arriving in front of the house, he couldn't believe, what he saw. The whole property was a total mess. Michael's answer was also straight, "I won't let something like this happen to me," decided Michael. He straightaway grabbed with his hands the next available solid stick, demanding that the people in his house better leave his property on the spot.

As nobody showed up nor wanted to move out, Michael decided, "If you don't listen, then I'll teach you the lesson of your lifetime. I didn't risk my life and the one of my family's to come home so that others could take advantage of it and lead a lazy life in my home. Get out now, or I kick you out."

Nobody wanted to listen to what Michael had said. It could last however only as long as the solid wooden stick of Michael came into action. At first, Michael experienced resistance with chairs flying through the air. Michael defended himself as much as he could until the other side realized that it was better to give up before more damage would occur. Michael didn't let to go until the last gypsy had left his house. To respond more friendly didn't want to work. Michael had suffered enough lately not so much that some vagrants could add more trouble.

The small local police station of Kleinschelken was not occupied all the time. Michael didn't expect any help from that side. Too many interests could have collided over the past and present.

Romania was about to change its political establishment to communism after Russia had invaded the country. Michael avoided people, especially those close to government authorities, as much as he could. The risk to become recognized from the Russian side was still too big.

To have finally regained his home, Michael had to think about how to go further. He couldn't understand what other people thought when they destroyed somebody else's property right into a pigsty. All that was left for Michael was his family. The whereabouts of his family members in such troublesome times was only possible through previously maintained contacts.

The sudden presence of Michael had, however, spread like a wildfire, less out of the curiosity but more out of responsibility for each other, as far as it had been possible. After the challenges Michael had experienced during his escape from Siberia, he was more or less a broken man than he could ever have imagined. While he connected to his relatives and friends, Michael didn't only receive help with food but also messages about the remainder of his own family. In these endeavors, the pastor became a central person. Michael also received from him the whereabouts of his son, Martin. Was it natural that people without children from a major town like Hermannstadt had taken care of Little Martin?

The district principal town of Mediasch played a role there, too. The community had established a home where children who had lost their parents found care. Little Martin must have especially pleased one helping hand because during his potty business, his only interest became the stories of the lady, completely forgetting why he was sitting on the pot. Instead, he held firmly on to the hand of this auntie, who became a long road in Little Martin's life.

The road lead also to Hermannstadt. The Kleinschelken pastor had found out where Little Martin has found a new home. Michael preferred to first look for the whereabouts of Little Martin before finding out where his older son also named Michael was. His son Michael had found a home within the family, even when it wasn't in the village of Kleinschelken.

The visit of Michael in Hermannstadt went very much differently than what he could have dreamed of. Around the countryside, the population became deeply insecure. The ongoing war made no halt in front of anybody's house door. As Michael, the father, finally found the courage and knocked gently at the door of the given address in Hermannstadt, he received only rejection, "Go to the hell you, peasant idiot. There is nobody for you here!"

Michael couldn't believe what he had heard. There was no answer for it, walking again away from the address he could only shake his head. What next? That question followed him all his life. He also asked himself how could there be people who have their way regardless of the others, when the latter have to struggle. Michael could find the answer to it during his lifetime. He was only sure about one thing: Life had to continue anyway when looking back at what he already had gone through in his life.

The war still determined everybody's life, whether one was a peasant, citizen from a city or somebody else. They all received the same treatment, regardless of where they originated from. Siberia added quite a number of experiences to Michael. He was under no circumstances prepared to end up again in the hands of war mongrels, no matter which nationality they belong to. The best place was still at home in the little village of Kleinschelken, where less conflict of interest took place.

A new life started for Michael at home with hardly any hope for a better future. Daily necessities kept everybody very busy, like a condemnation to a life that had stopped. Hardly any change occurred in this situation of many lives. Michael's visit to Hermannstadt had unexpected consequences. The arrival of Michael spread unstoppably within this close community of the *Siebenbürger Sachsen*. The community kept close together and didn't sell out one of their own. Help during these times was most important.

WAY SEPARATION DOESN'T STOP

So, it also happened that the couple who had taken care of Little Martin couldn't resist to let Michael see his son for a photo. The book cover image goes back to this occasion. From this moment on, the paths of Little Martin and his father, Michael, went into different directions. They were not asked whether they liked it or not.

Michael must have somehow found a new way to go on with his life. Was it good or not that Little Martin ended up in the care of strange hands?

The fate of the other son was also hanging in a balance between family and friends, who could only care for a young life as it was possible at the time. Despite the war and political uncertainties, the life had to continue no matter what the circumstances were.

Russia was already determined at that time to show its military might in Romania. It did mean for Michael to remain as little as possible noticeable even within the community of his own village.

The fate of the second son, Little Martin, was sealed away from Kleinschelken in a place called Busteni, in the middle of the southern Carpathian Mountains.

A manufacturing initiative of paper supported by private hands and the government created there for Little Martin's new parents a source of wealth, even if it lasted only for a short time.

The American military became, at that time, already "helpful" in Romania, aiming to get rid of the Nazi presence. Let's stick to something better known within this biographical novel, namely closer at home in Kleinschelken.

How would Michael's escape from Siberia compare with another continued escape in a life? Once an escapee, always an escapee? In any case, two paths had come from it: One way back at home in Kleinschelken and the other one away from it.

Let's remain still in Kleinschelken and see what had happened in and around Michael's family home. The other path out of Busteni in the Carpathian Mountains will continue at a later stage in this novel.

REGAIN KLEINSCHELKEN

It has never been an easy task for somebody to rebuild a life. Therefore, it became important for Michael to maintain courage and let enough time to pass to see what is possible.

Back at home, Michael also learned that the sister of his wife, Elisabeth, still experienced the hardship of an imprisonment in Siberia. After three years, she came home again. Meanwhile for Michael, time passed in a wait-and- see mode. The war time also stripped any initiative from all. Despite Elisabeth being cut off for three years from contacts, she returned home to Kleinschelken against all odds. Home also had for her magical powers. Her life in Siberia was so inhumane that no words could describe such a suffering. A young woman like Elisabeth experienced especially bad times. Why can people do so much wrong to each other? In those years, everything imaginable Elisabeth had experienced. Unfortunately, a tragedy of this dimension struck most people with silence during the rest of their lives until death.

A large number of war prisoners from Siberia didn't return home alive. Some couldn't find any comfort at home on which to rebuild a life. Elisabeth could, however, still remember her home where her sister Sara and husband Michael also called their home in Kleinschelken. The family also became for her the last anchor.

Where more than one person could find hope, new ways for life found ground. Not only man belongs to a family but the helpful driving force of a wife, too. This way both, Elisabeth and Michael, pulled together for a possible new beginning in their life. To a family belong also children. The two sons, Michael Jr. and Martin had somehow found a home. Only in coming years, it became evident that the fate of Michael turned into a more difficult one, although he remained in his native country, Transylvania. Every life looks like a lucky draw. When we look into a future, we can never really know what lies ahead.

The paths from Kleinschelken and Busteni separated the family members from each other for almost a whole lifetime. In Kleinschelken, the communist regime had put the brakes on for new developing ways. A connection to the ruling party enabled only some individuals to lead a reasonable life. All the others had to pay for it. As nothing was available anyway, not much was left for the majority of the population.

Michael had the courage with his new wife, the sister of his late wife Sara, to extend the family with four other children. It could also have been regarded here that only challenges brought real strength out. The family remained united because more hands can always manage more than only single ones. The modest life in Kleinschelken spared its villagers much of foreign interferences because the freedom of religion ruled unopposed; however, nothing for somebody who was after the power and money. The church fortress of the Kleinschelken village also proved because it had withstood over centuries all the interferences from outside and during war times. People came and left, but only the religious belief remained.

Elisabeth's skillful hands managed to return the daily family life to some normality, which mainly started with the endless small things. Neither surplus nor luxury was around, which was, however, enough to stay basically healthy. After a few years, a more regular life could again be established according to a proven recipe of divided tasks: The wife looks after the internal affairs; the husband after the external ones. If we give them the names of a home secretary and a foreign minister, the foreign minister is a man proud of his wine cellar under the house with wooden barrels filled with his own wine and schnapps. This wine culture also found appreciation outside the one's own house walls or village. An unwritten custom, however, was around that the real good wine remained at home and in the family, among friends and important relatives. The less cultivated wine was considered good enough for city people and other strangers. Wine for the city represented a strong binding element with the countryside. For that reason, it was important that this wine remained highly regarded.

At a peasant's home, it was also a tradition to keep smoked bacon in the house because bacon with a glass of schnapps from one's own barrel didn't only help with digestion but also the well-being within the community. Even in the roof trusses of the church fortresses waited in its defense galleries wheat bundles hanging together with smoked bacon from every peasant's home.

The villagers then played the waiting game and gave their support when a defense was needed, starving the enemy out. Enemy raids took quite often away whatever they liked from the community. Until recently, this defense readiness had worked over eight hundred years already. The inner center of the church received care and love, an image which represents a more contended life with the faith. The Transylvanian Saxons have always been and still are strong believers in the Lutheran church. A first migration to the area of today's Transylvania from the area surrounding today's Luxembourg took place during the twelfth century from the area surrounding today's Luxembourg. Then much later, under the rule of Maria Theresa, the Protestants of Austria were expelled, which prompted a second settlement to Transylvania. Despite all the challenges in the past, the Siebenbürger Saxons preserved their unity until the arrival of the communism in Romania. Difficult situations were not only demanding but called for strength. A strong belief in tradition always contributed to a unity, so it could continue in great cultural expressions. How long it will last into the future remains to be seen.

28

BUSTENI, A NEW WAY

One move away from tradition has been already seen in Busteni, a place located in the Southern Carpathian Mountains, where Little Martin was brought. A short but sweet time allowed the freshly baked family to stay and enjoy their life until Russia demanded, "Out with the Nazi military together with the American protecting forces!" An escape again became the answer if someone didn't want to become a target. Wanted or not, the new parents of Little Martin were in a hurry to start their own escape. There was no time to even think or plan something ahead. A freight train didn't wait at the local station for a regular departure. For whomever the word, *escape,* reached appeared immediately at the station to catch the last train going to the west.

How could it happen and still is at present that the bad can win the upper hand? It was no surprise that the escape of well-situated people spread even secretly. Shortly after the master of the house arrived at the station, he returned once more to the house in a hurry to collect at least some blankets to put on to the timber floor of the train carriage. All he could find, without inviting anybody in, were hobos who had already forcibly entered the house. A return to the station became more pressing as the train was not specially waiting for somebody.

The time made people equals. The crowd already congested in the carriages looked rather poor from the start. Between each carriage, a guard, an American soldier with a gun, had taken his position. More in a hurry than anything else, the train took off, pulled by a steam engine. Somebody must have had a say about everything that happened there. The peaks of the Carpathian Mountains looked uninterested at this escape. One difference that marked this occasion was that the American occupying forces at least allowed Transylvanians from Busteni to get out from there to the west with them. Who there was involved in the decision-making remained under the carpet. One difference from *Ochotska Sibir* was that there, the imprisonment reigned firmly over the escapees; whereas under that command a door was left open with hope and freedom to the west. What really happened is a part of another very long story. This novel shall tell from here on only essential steps in the life of Little Martin, which could be regarded as a continuation of an escape from who knows where. Only life will be able to tell! One central theme remains: The war causes only a great deal of trouble for everybody.

How did this journey on board of a train go for Little Martin? Martin was still too little to comprehend what happened to him and around him. Luck was most in demand there because what happened was in the hands of others whom nobody knew. Doesn't it speak clearly enough against a war? Stories helped wake memories later. If we want to learn something at all, it would become necessary to seek new ways with the help of the past, because no past can be ignored and thrown overboard.

That escape also turned out to something not really wishful. But by the same token we've to accept that plans in life rarely work out to an undisputed satisfaction. In this novel, the author looks on behalf of the reader for avenues that do not end up in dead-end roads, but as it is also said, "All roads lead to Rome" which means that everything in life is connected to each other.

This continued escape provided its own difficulties, too. How much was it destined that Little Martin arrived on that road and not another one? The own interest of a family idea with this child determined the road direction in this novel. Back at the local orphanage in Mediasch, an agreement was reached by which the new parents exchanged "ownership" of Little Martin with money. On his first and last visit to his native country much later in 1978, all this was confirmed by Martin's own family in a face-to-face meeting.

The events of this escape on a freight train were still under American control. Most of all, it could be said that it was anything else than a pleasant one. The duration of this "journey" only created some not previously known hardships for many passengers. Hunger again became one of the first "messengers". The military control personnel on the otherhand had more than enough food, even if it was tinned ones. Already the smell of it misled many of the passengers into a desperate action to pull a half finished tin through a door gap into the carriage. A misunderstanding was quickly on hand so that the control man saw the security endangered, therefore responding as he was told: Shoot the bastard. To resolve this action, the train stopped for a moment and the offender was removed from the train.

It was not to be the only disturbance during that escape. The closer the train arrived at the Austrian border, the more they were facing the actions of the war. Allied Airforces dropped bombs on the train. The steam engine with its driver was hit, and as a result, the train had to stop. The passengers were ordered to escape for their own protection to the close by fields close-by. According to later reports, Martin found protection underneath his new mother while lying flat on the ground. That time luck had decided for Little Martin, and much of such luck became necessary for his life to continue.

Sometime later, the train moved again with the help from the Austrian border. Why that escape took place during the winter time remained a mystery on an unwritten piece of paper. However, one fact remained: During the winter, everything appeared to be more difficult. The welcome in the west by Austria was more "cold" than anything else. The water for the steam engine was not yet frozen but cold enough to give a great shock to the poor escapees because they were not clean enough for the Austrians. Nobody had time to wonder what was going on. The only answer became: Everything had to go on from there.

NOTIFICATIONS FROM THE WEST

To keep going was a difficult answer, especially during war times, when much had already been reduced to rubble. The answer was left with every individual. By coincidence, Martin's new family already had connections in Germany, which gained some importance. The escape didn't want to come to an end yet. Other homes included the war and the years afterwards: Weilderstadt (J.Keppler place), Rotenbach (in Enz river valley), Weissenstein (near Pforzheim), Ettlingen (near Karlsruhe)— Little Martin started to remember his own life in these places.

    The world could be regarded lucky to still have children. They are the ones who could not comprehend the extent of a misery the Second World War had inflicted on all people. To a large extent, it was the children who could find some room for positive memories. All was not only bad for somebody who had saved some leftovers with healthy humor. One could then also see farther than the length of one's own nose. Food cards became a symbol of that time. They tried to control the little that was left with food. The farmers in many areas of Germany didn't need to really tighten their belts as much. The food cards were, by far, not enough for most people who had to listen to the questions of a few donors, such as: What have you got for me? That "game" was unequal and unfair.

Years later the new parents of Little Martin were able to turn the tables when they visited some of the earlier accommodations with their own car, also saying good day without missing to pull out of their memory box: "What have you got for us?" The other side had at that time no answers anymore but were left where they had been all the time. That, however, didn't contribute to a better understanding, because in their eyes refugees remained refugees.

Another occasion left more room for humor as well. Everything was still almost missing after the war. In Rotenbach on the *Gänsbrunnen Wiese* (Geesewell Meadows) the heaps of rubble in the bombed cities were away far enough. The administration of the municipalities found some work, although not much had to be administered at all. One task should have become to find out who needed a simple cart on wheels and should be allowed to put an application in.

When the question about the cart was raised at home, Little Martin was all ears. Martin must have had a better memory at that time than all the others. Not much later, Little Martin reminded his parents, "When are we going to receive the cart on wheels?"

The parents had almost forgotten about it but said in a hurry, "We are asking again." Time had to go past again. Another time, when Little Martin asked for the whereabouts of the cart, the answer was, "It will be a *rutscherle*, something a bit smaller than a cart on wheels."

"Does a rutscherle also have four wheels?" asked Little Martin.

"A *rutscherle* does not have four wheels but only two," was the father's answer.

Little Martin tried to figure out what this difference of wheel numbers could mean. He was not prepared to let much time go before he repeatedly asked about the cart on two wheels.

Difficult times have always asked for divided attention for other things, too. The result for the inquiry on the two-wheel cart finally became that there will be no cart with two wheels either. The whole thing was an "error". Little Martin listened carefully to what has been said and asked once more disappointedly, "How many wheels does an error have?" Those words accompanied many more memories throughout Little Martin's lifetime.

Whether a refugee or not, the movements didn't want to disappear for Little Martin. How much did his fate follow the appeal, "A boat is secure in a harbour, but is not its destination" by Paulo Coelho, a Brazilian Author.

After the war, Germany challenged its remaining citizens fundamentally with a rebuilding. The social stigma of a refugee didn't want to go away on its own, especially when the "old school" that dated back to the "good old times" had its say. Little Martin had to follow these footsteps. A missing link to a changed time in the new environment caused the harsh behaviour of a family circle, even in a small one: 1. You are not allowed to speak unless you are asked. 2. If you don't do what we demand, we won't help you. 3. Proper eating requires the arms close to the body and not the elbows sticking out on both sides. 4. Put these few books under your upper arms, so you can better understand, and make sure you don't drop the books. 5. when I say the mountain is not 1500 metres high, then that's it. I give you no permission to look at the map! 6. Also, the Finnish are decent ones, too (This was said in front of the author's future wife, Arja, who is from Finland) and it went so on and so forth.

In Transylvania, the family of Michael tried to do their best in the life with smaller steps. They were preoccupied enough with their own fate. The governing communist authorities kept everybody insecure for many years even after the war. The little village of Kleinschelken became much less disrupted from outside interferences because of its hidden position in the countryside. However, a recovery from the war time took much longer than in the West of Germany.

A turning point in Martin's life, who by then could not be called little anymore, didn't fail to change in time. All in all, the home of Transylvania was denied him for a long time during his life in Germany. It became more than obvious that he had a lot of luck; therefore, an abundance of experiences came with it, too. Probably typical for the son of the peasant, Michael, that he persistently was seeking his own way in life. A character he obviously inherited from his father, Michael.

The town of Ettlingen became the place for Martin to pursue his education goals, which started with an apprenticeship as a toolmaker. Parallel to it, he studied an engineer course to become independent from home as soon as possible. Every available spare hour, Martin also helped with the construction of the family home in Ettlingen. One special item received Martin's skilled attention; namely, the letter box that he elevated into an art form with wrought iron and shiny hammered copper, inside and outside the house wall. What Martin couldn't know then that only the head of the household had the right to attend to the post deliveries. This might sound insignificant; however, much importance would come of it in the later years.

Before this novel goes back to this detail, much else had happened since in Martin's life: At Abendgymnasium in Karlsruhe, he fulfilled the requirements for the *Abitur*. He visited, with own initiatives and own efforts, the Ruperto Carola, University of Heidelberg until the Baader-Meinhoff student troubles during the end of the 1960s brought the university to a standstill. Martin had enough from this direction. He had befriended Arja in Finland, who had also joined Martin in Heidelberg for her studies. A turning point came when they both pulled some strings together to get married in Finland. Attempts to gain some foothold in Germany on their own didn't work out for this adventurous young couple.

On the other hand, in Finland, they faced different conditions. Earlier experiences of Martin's adventures opened both their views further.

SOUTH AFRICA

South Africa came next in line. Based on his education, experiences, and skills, South Africa financed the couple and their already three children to come to the country.

The family experienced three very nice and successful years in South Africa. However, it needs to be added that the political situation in the 1970s changed a lot in the country. It was in South Africa that the family life of Martin started to catch up with the past. A handwritten letter from his father, Michael, found its way to his son, Martin, with the official help of the Red Cross, after the mail in the letter box in Ettlingen couldn't disappear anymore. Michael had searched all those years for the whereabouts of his son, Martin. The Red Cross found Martin only after he had left the country, and nobody could stop the letter anymore.

The letter started with: Finally, I have found, after so many years, my stolen son again. All the details surrounding this occasion is a story of its own. Martin's wife, Arja, ought to have said that it is the first time that she has seen Martin cry.

Another turning point had arrived there. Could it become a trigger for another escape? As nice as the fresh start in South Africa might have been, it turned so quickly under the pressure of unjust apartheid conditions. Martin and his family had an easy-going arrival in South Africa, leaving the country, however, proved to be much more difficult. Family connection in Brazil, therefore, invited us to go to Brazil.

BRAZIL

After a good preparation, this adventure succeeded. What was experienced by Martin and his family was a mixture of both good and bad. Far enough from the population centers, they established on their own property a life of relative freedom they were looking for. Surrounding conditions dangerously changed their perceptions. The Portuguese language was not a problem; furthermore, plenty of qualified engineering work was available. Martin also had a good relationship with people that resulted in a good professional position; however, extreme social conditions reaching to unimaginable deprivation to ruthless wealth and dangerous health conditions, among others made their family rethink about their future in Brazil. To get out of Brazil that was under the military rule was virtually impossible. However, Martin's family made it possible with a unique expedition throughout the whole South American continent with a brand-new car and a trailer behind. Only with far reaching adaptability to the present other military dictatorships in the South American continent made it even possible to succeed in this undertaking. On that tour, they met one Japanese bicycle rider who travelled around the world and was also beating all the odds as Martin, Arja, and their four children, including their dog, a German shepherd.

EUROPE & TRANSYLVANIA

One particular goal also determined this escape-tour. As soon as the family had arrived in Europe, they wanted to visit Martin's father Michael and his family in Kleinschelken at the first opportunity. Once more, the family, all six members including Max the German shepherd, had luck on their side when returning to Europe from Brazil were happy and healthy.

Back in Germany, the task was to find a way back into that society. The first move led the wife, Arja, to Finland with their four children. Her mother, Tysse, travelled to Stockholm, Sweden, to meet her daughter and grandchildren earlier. After six years away from Europe, it was no doubt that the welcome was a heartfelt one. The biggest problem was not the dog, but the four children in Germany but not at all in Finland! To overcome this problem, it was left for the others to sort out the future without children.

In the following summer, Martin could take holidays from his work in the Stuttgart area and follow the goal to meet his Transylvanian family. Typical for Europe, the masses found themselves held up in a dense road traffic. Was it a modern escape from a daily life? In Martin's case, it could be regarded as a family reunion because ways of an escape must not necessarily lead to a separation, as long as hope remained an essential part of it.

On the way to Romania, differences in governing a country didn't fail to present itself. Mainly in Romania, visitors awaited only strict control measures. The children and the dog in the car, however, gave no cause for suspicion. In the flat meadow countryside mixed with forest islands, the road led through a hilly countryside to the western part of Transylvania at the start of the journey. It was not a "road to Rome", but to Martin's home, the village of Kleinschelken. In the heartland of Transylvania (Siebenbürgen) traffic, the road around the cities of Hermannstadt and Mediasch consisted mainly of rural traffic with people mainly on foot. A foreign car model drew particular attention not only to local people but to proud geese, which walked on the side of the road. It was recommended to take special attention because cars were still rarely seen on the road.

Many holes on the road to the first address of a brother in Eibesdorf welcomed the driver. Only in the village did the road turn out smooth. Could it have been a stumbling point also for the communism to visit the village?

Typically for these villages were the houses that were built united in a row on both sides of a road, which allowed one to usually enter through large individual gates in each backyard. Nobody could have been seen on the road. An elderly woman dressed in black had taken a seat in front of a house on a few steps. Martin stopped the car in front of the elderly woman. Martin's cautious approach in the German language was replied naturally in German, too.

"Yes, Hans lives just around the corner on the left side of the road." Everything was clear and the doors were open.

The family was welcomed as friendly as someone could only wish if both sides had known each other all their lives. The visit got extended in the neighborhood with the brother's parents in law. The father-in-law was employed by the government police (Miliz). Normally, all visitors would seek accommodation in a government hotel. The reference of the police helped such that nobody could have argued that the family had been accommodated by relatives. A visit from the West was considered well-to-do people . A car could, especially, give the wrong impression too easily. The consume and simple life were not yet around that time. It emerged more clearly in the coming years. There and in the West, everybody had to work hard for a reasonable existence. Some people somehow managed access to goods from the west, as everybody could see with own eyes. However, everything in Transylvania also had its own price, even when the bill turned much later up.

It was not now a question of an outstanding bill. The first contact could neither stop a visit to Kleinschelken, where so much had happened in the past. At the entrance of the Kockel valley, huge piles of mining activities had left a question mark as to who were really the winners or losers. The government made also sure that they didn't end on the losers' bench. The peasants around the area were the ones who had to deal with the problems caused by mining. Why, most of the time, people wake up after the damage had been done should not be the subject of this novel.

KLEINSCHELKEN AGAIN

More important was to continue the visit to Kleinschelken, on the road which went past the mining area in a more or less safe distance. Later, the two church towers announced their hidden position between green hills where the road was leading to. The river Kockel had also found its way through a deeply washed-out river bed, standing out alone in the middle of row houses, leaving appropriate space around the church fortress. To find the parents' home was an easy and quick task as everybody knew each other well enough.

    A circle from the past into the present came there to a close. As Michael, the father, went exactly on June 22 in 1941 in the morning to his section of the field on foot, so he returned that day home again on foot. The arrival of Martin and his family in Kleinschelken hadn't reach him yet. After a first welcome in the house by Elisabeth, the mother, and three brothers and a sister took place on a Saturday, when somebody would most likely be at home. Martin was asked to cross the Kockel riverbed and walk to the other side. He had not yet arrived on the opposite hillside when a man appeared from the field work with a long hoe over his shoulder. He, the father, Michael and the son, Martin, didn't need to come much closer when the father recognized the son, although so much time had separated them from each other. On the last steps, they hurried to get closer to each other. No words were said, only a heartfelt hug and arms around each other, even the eyes couldn't meet. They both, father and son, remained silent, continuing their way together home. The moment was so exciting that not even the tears could be stopped.

The car was still waiting in front of the closed gate. Michael demanded straightaway to bring the car into the yard, so no wrong impressions could circulate. In the center of the arched gate wings, which were in a line with the other house fronts, a support base for the gates stuck a fraction out too much. The Brazilian Chevrolet station wagon could not clear this obstacle enough to be driven into the yard. A number of wooden planks helped to bring the car quickly away from the sight of too curious onlookers.

When the car had also been looked after, nothing prevented everybody to get to know each other better. Too many years had passed before. Michael was keen to show his wine cellar under the house, which was full of wooden barrels filled with his own wine and schnapps, all nicely put on brick supports. Michael must have known that in wine there is truth (*In vino est veritas*). His house wine helped to free everybody's tongue to bring as many words out as possible. The welcome was friendly and open, kept in reasonable bounds. No wonder, because too much time had already gone to catch up with the past only in a few moments. The growing children caused no problems when it came to clean the table up. Before moving farther and visiting other family members and friends in Kleinschelken and farther away, Martin's eldest son, Risto, cleaned some of the glasses up. The result came as no surprise that at least one, namely Risto, got drunk for the first time but probably not the last time in his life.

Could there be no better proof delivered of the house wine's quality? The son's early love for drops of wine prompted Martin's wife to stay at home in Kleinschelken, while the others moved on.

Excursions, sightseeing, and even playing football on green grass fields against the impressive silhouette of the Carpathian Mountain peaks, which were covered higher up in white permanent snow fields, were included. Entertainments and visiting a restaurant were still uncommon; that's why Martin couldn't invite the family for dinner to a restaurant. Communism controlled everything, and private initiatives were not allowed.

Among many other activities and moves, the family picked up, Martin's brother Michael in Heltau, near Hermannstadt, so that he could be part of the family meeting, too. That move, unfortunately, was not a very pleasant one. The time and difficult circumstances didn't allow what anybody was hoping for. Out of a more modest hidden position Michael, the brother, worked hard to receive attention by being helpful all the time to family members and friends. Perhaps, he almost forgot himself when he helped somebody to renovate his flat completely. Very bad luck caught with him up as he entered the flat and switched the light on; everything around him exploded because the gas stove wasn't switched off properly. As a result, Michael, the brother, suffered burns on his skin all over the entire body. With more luck than nothing else, he overcame this bad luck that marked him for the rest of his life.

The brother, Michael's life had to continue after the incident, too. The whole family was again united at home in Kleinschelken. Michael, the brother, received his due attention from everybody. Although Martin and Michael were brothers, to reconnect with the past as well as future during the short reunion didn't turn out as well as Martin had hoped for. In general, it could be said that the family reunion was friendly and heartfelt. Even Martin's wife from Finland received unreserved attention from everybody, without forgetting that she also spoke fluently German.

The accommodation of the family in the father, Michael's home was a clear one, "When my son comes home with his family, the communism has nothing to say!" The isolation in the small village of Kleinschelken, good contacts with all neighbors reached farther beyond the village and made it possible to bypass the government's regulations, which was every foreigner had to stay in hotels provided by the government. In that regard, Michael, the father, was not prepared, under any circumstances, to change his determination. It is no wonder that he could leave Siberia behind. The time, however, reminded that everything must also find its end. In Transylvania, life also asked for continuation, even under difficult conditions that communism tried to maintain. Time told people to keep their mouths shut, pretending to conform with everything and keep going from one day to the next one.

"ESCAPE" FROM KLEINSCHELKEN

The time for the first visit of Martin with his family at home in Kleinschelken had its strings attached, namely that no holiday can last forever. The goodbyes happened suddenly as if chickens got frightened in their own yard. It was decided in a hurry that another brother took a seat in the car, while Martin and his family headed back to Germany. If it were destined to fail or not, the locals ought to have known better than Martin that the brother left his family behind in Kleinschelken, hoping his escape to Germany with Martin would succeed so that he and his family could gain freedom, too. That situation explained more or less why during the farewell from the parental home in Kleinschelken, one couldn't see tears in everybody's eyes. The hope to see each other soon again must have been greater. To speak on behalf of Martin, he relied on the family in Kleinschelken with the decision. As it proved not long after, the plan became a failure.

The area around the passage when leaving Transylvania to the West received no particular attention anymore. All seven in the car reached the border town of Timisoara (Temeschwar) next to Yugoslavia in a short time, uninterrupted for the time being. However, an interruption in front of the hotel for tourists caught up with the returning visitors.

The brother left the car on his own and spoke in the Romanian language to some official in a uniform. The course of that journey went wrong from that moment on. When the brother returned to the car and took his seat again. The man the brother spoke to, most probably a security personnel, was tasked to report anything suspicious to his higher authorities.

Martin, the driver, became very uncertain about continuing the tour under these circumstances, especially when the brother began to hide under the back seat of the car. Farther away, a spy dome appeared on the horizon, which certainly kept an eye on the surroundings. As almost could be predicted, just before the border line, a police officer came in front of the car, signalling that the driver move to the side. By then, Martin, the driver, knew well enough that something had gone wrong. In a hurry, he passed on the message to his brother, "Tell only the truth!"

Because contradictions would have made the case rather more difficult. All the doors of the car were opened, and armed guards ordered all the passengers to follow them into the nearby building. The brother was, however, treated separately because he was declared the main culprit, as he was the only one who spoke the Romanian language. What happened to the car in the meanwhile, the driver had no idea. The German shepherd was fortunately left with Martin and his family in a separate room.

The border control personnel kept themselves busy with enquiries, although none of the family members had enough knowledge to communicate in the Romanian language. It must be admitted that the case could by no means be called a normal one. It was Martin's own mistake to become trapped in a communistic power "machinery".

One of the next steps hit Martin with a surprise. An officer demanded the car keys, sat on the driver's seat, allowing Martin to watch him drive from the front passenger seat. Off went the tour back to Timisoara (Temeschwar) and how this new driver enjoyed driving the car! The police officer was driving as fast as he could. What happened to Martin's brother was left in the dark. The only hope remained that he didn't already cop the usual corporal punishment in the beginning. The car driven by the Romanian border official stopped exactly in front of the tourist hotel, where an enquiry was previously made. The hotel now became the place for the family to stay on their own expense!

No matter what the present situation was going to look like, Martin himself was fully aware that the whole family had arrived in a dangerous situation. The only question left was how to get out of the tough spot again. It had to be on a Saturday, just in the beginning of a weekend, when everybody was heading for a more peaceful weekend. Martin managed to get into a necessary contact with the German ambassador over the phone. Speaking in French and not Romanian language, Martin managed to get ahold of him. The ambassador was reacting surprisingly quickly in favor of Martin, before heading into the weekend. He even managed to get into a contact with the local judges' institution, as Martin experienced in further developments.

Otherwise, the family had the "great privilege" to be accommodated in a first-class hotel room on their own expense (as already mentioned) however, under strict conditions not to leave their hotel room. The weekend passed for the family in a very slow motion while uncertainty was hanging above their heads. One interruption took place when a uniformed officer asked Martin to follow him into the latter's car, which was waiting in front of the hotel. The car obviously drove to the town center with the officer driving the car. Among other big buildings, one building turned out to be a courthouse.

JURISDICTION IN ROMANIA

Martin didn't follow the driver into the building but instead another uniformed person. The layout of the building's interior had rows of seats in a half circle and a long table in front of it, which indicated that it was a court house. One seat was assigned for Martin while one gentleman dressed in a judicial black toga raised his voice behind the front table, interestingly in the French language. Martin could fluently deliver his answers in French. Judging the reaction from the judicial side, Martin's answers must have been well received. He simply expressed his sorrow to have unknowingly violated the Romanian legislation.

The meeting then came quickly to an end. This time, Martin was driving the car back to the hotel, under the supervision of a custom's official with the request to bring the whole family to the car and wait to be driven by the officially appointed Romanian driver back to the border. The family, including the German shepherd, silently watched what was going to happen. Right in front of the lowered border barrier, the official person went out of the car, handed the car keys to Martin, while somebody else raised the border barrier, indicating to keep driving farther. Straight after the car had passed the border barrier, it was closed again.

What had been behind all of that, one could only have guessed. It was important that the family could leave Romania without the danger of an imprisonment. The German deputy consul in Bucharest obviously must have done his part of the job well. Only much later, Martin received a notification from the family in Transylvania that the brother had arrived at home without serious implications. One bitter aftertaste, however, remained that Martin's family was barred from entering Romania again for another ten years. Was that "exercise" worthwhile at all? Martin's family must have forgotten that they had entered Romania, which was governed at that time under strict communistic rules. In addition, came the fact that the brother, who wanted to join the family to go to Germany, was unwisely handled.

At the end, it still emerged that, "all is well that ends well". Martin had to hurry returning back with the car to which they called their home for the time being because the holidays had rapidly come to an end. Life in Transylvania, like in Germany, had to continue. Both sides were left with daily challenges, however of a very different nature. The communist government suppressed the Lutheran religion in the close communities of Transylvania (Siebenbürgen) to an extent that they started bulldozing these old traditional communities in order to gain total control, moving them out of their individual environment into high-rise buildings. The Saxons of Transylvania didn't watch it for long. They revolted united against the government and abolished the injustice by killing the communist leader, Ceausescu, in particular his wife who really pulled the strings.

THE FURTHER WAY

In West Germany much was different at that time. Whether it was for better or worse, it was left to individuals find out for themselves. Martin encountered the problem with his four children. Leading responsible work, yes, but accommodation for the family, no. The family could already look back to conditions they experienced in Finland, South Africa, and Brazil. The decision of finding other shores didn't fail to materialize since the experiences told that there were still better ways of leading a life. Could this have been called another escape from an unwanted reality?

As an independent family, they regarded themselves still free to make their own decisions. Luckily, people are different also in ways that some are seeking mainly comfort, security through means of consume, while there are also others who lead their lives making their own decisions.

In the case of Martin's family, a new way led, as far as it only could be, to Australia. The Australian government wanted to have Martin's family in the country. The government paid for the move. It ought to last the whole lifetime, which started in August 1981. A stumbling point, however, remained: The ten-year ban of Martin's family to enter the Romanian territory. It turned especially sad as during that time

Father Michael passed away in Kleinschelken, much too early. No doubt the war imprisonment had left its marks also with him. His memory lives on in the family and very much so in this novel, which his son, Martin, has dedicated to his father, Michael.

The author hopes that readers' interests could connect to the author's efforts in this novel. Many ways exist in a life; they all have evolved from different "branches" of a life's tree. We are challenged by abysses, if committed or not. It is also what the words, "All roads lead to Rome" mean. We only need to have the courage and recognize the tasks in a life, mainly with activities, and not only wait and see what is going to happen. It is the only way to give life a sense of meaning. Faith is also given here a role of building bridges to other lives.